Si 's
s
e

Michael Smith's
Simple Dinner Parties
for busy people

London
Victor Gollancz Ltd
1988

First published in Great Britain in 1988
by Victor Gollancz Ltd
14 Henrietta Street London WC2E 8QJ

© 1988 by Michael Smith

British Library Cataloguing in Publication Data
Smith, Michael
    Michael Smith's simple dinner parties for
    busy people.
    1. Food—Recipes
    I. Title
    641.5

    ISBN 0-575-04073-4

The recipes for Savoury Butters on pp. 139–40
are published by kind permission of Macmillan
and are taken from *Michael Smith's Afternoon Tea Book*

Photoset in Great Britain by
Rowland Phototypesetting Ltd, Bury St Edmunds, Suffolk
and printed and bound in Singapore
by Imago Publishing Ltd

Contents

Introduction

Contents

Introduction

There can be nothing more satisfying than to survive throwing a dinner party and to come through intact. The greatest compliment you can pay anyone is to ask them into your house and to feed them no matter how simply.

For many, to ask friends to dinner can be daunting to say the least. There's no problem if you enjoy cooking and can cook. But what if your technique is limited? How do you cope?

The inspiration for this collection of recipes springs from my many and various friends: hard-working, food-loving, restaurant-going, often totally absorbed in a life of music and the arts, nothing if not sociable, but not much given to spending precious hours in the kitchen. Many are single, all are style-conscious. Those who are opera-lovers either perform the music or else linger in the concert hall until the last note has drifted away from the gods, before hurrying home to relive with fellow devotees the finer points of the performance. They like to do this round a table set with fine food and wine. Other friends wrestle with demanding jobs and equally demanding families, yet still, at the end of a hard day and despite the fact that the childminder has left, love to entertain at home.

They ask what should they cook, how much can it be prepared in advance, in fact, how can they cope with the whole spectrum of entertaining from table-setting to washing up, whilst still having time to relax and enjoy their friends' company, which is, after all, the whole object of the exercise?

Their discerning palates have been nurtured and refined by the exotic fare offered by the country's new gamut of restaurants, so that the simple grilled lamb cutlet served with a salad, followed by French bread and Brie, which *can* be assembled without loss of equilibrium, is, frankly, boring, if served more than once or so.

The problem is that, recognising the desirable intimacy of socialising at home, these and many other busy people have nevertheless not had time to acquire gradually the requisite culinary skills and do not now have the time or inclination to go back to basics, to begin at the beginning. It reminds me of when I was a stripling of twenty years and decided to have a go at playing the piano again but I wasn't at all interested in scales, I wanted to play Haydn, Brahms and Mozart. Fortunately, the legendary Fanny Waterman took me in hand, starting me from day one on the simple Haydn C Major Piano Concerto.

And so with cooking. Have your lesson on the foods you like to eat: produce a showpiece without necessarily making a basic roux or an elaborate stock; organise a full dinner menu without spending days in the kitchen, in fact, produce dinner within an hour or so of getting into the house, using recipes that have style, if not downright panache.

How This Book Works

The aim here is to provide a guiding hand to help you enjoy real cooking. The book is broadly organised into first courses, main dishes and desserts, the chapters within these sections each offering recipes, which allow a wide scope for menu planning, further varied by the suggestions for accompaniments given in the recipes themselves. All recipes are designed for a party of six.

It is always a good idea to read any recipe through to the end before starting to cook it but the recipes here have been consciously planned with advance preparation in mind, each one being sectioned off into 1. Advance preparation, 2. Pre-dinner and last-minute cooking, 3. Finishing touches and 4. Accompaniments.

Preparation and cooking times are given. As people work at differing speeds, an average is given to provide a rough idea of how long a dish will take. But read the instructions well in advance, as sometimes marinating or defrosting overnight is recommended.

The methods are written to give the uninitiated as much assistance as if the maestro were standing by your side, so that the usual bald instructions are augmented by a description of the sights, smells and even the sounds of the food as it cooks. If the butter will burn a little, I will tell you so, or if it will splutter before subsiding, this, too, I describe.

Behind the Scenes

So much for the workings of the recipes. This book also provides both the necessary basic elements and the fine-tuning, which, in the first case, will make your work in the kitchen run more smoothly and, in the second, will assist you in giving the all-important professional delivery to the finished dishes.

Using the right piece of equipment instantly reduces the frustration level in the preparation and cooking. My recipes are specific on this point and the various utensils are gathered together into a useful list on page 16. Hints and tips towards achieving the polished end-product are at the end under

'Basics': mostly seemingly-simple processes, such as separating an egg yolk, chopping an onion, skinning a tomato, which can be effected in moments when you know the right way but which otherwise can be a time-consuming stumbling-block.

Behind-the-scenes work is, of course, where organisation and planning pay the highest dividends. Fresh ingredients—meat, vegetables and fruit —need to be bought as near to the time of consumption as possible. So make a list and stagger your shopping, buying those ingredients which can be bought underripe first (e.g. cheese or avocado) and the delicate ones, such as fish and shellfish, last. If you are using frozen foods, I recommend a slow thawing in the bottom of the refrigerator. I do not make great use of a microwave cooker but it does have its use in the preparation of the accompanying vegetables and can aid the defrosting process.

Freshly grown herbs and a store cupboard stocked with fine quality oils, baking ingredients, dried herbs, spices and flavourings is an invaluable source of instantly-available subtleties to add the spice of individuality to your cooking. These are an integral part of my recipes and have been assembled on page 13 as a starter-pack for the novices and an aide-mémoire for those who already have some supplies.

Menu Planning

The cupboard is stocked, the pans are ready, the recipes await your decision—what will be your chosen menu? This is such a matter of individual preference and so vitally linked to the time and ingredients available, that the book is so organised as to allow you to make your own combinations. Bear in mind, though, the various facets of a successful *table d'hôte*. Balance is the *sine qua non*. Offset a rich main course, such as the 'Pan-Fried Breasts of Duckling in a Mustard and Rum Cream Sauce' with a plain starter and a fresh, sharp-tasting dessert. For example, preface the duck with a bowl of Avgolemono and conclude with the 'Compôte of Kumquats with Whisky'. This trio of courses would satisfy another important requirement: that of colour. Refresh the eye as well as the palate with colour changes, either from dish to dish or with carefully chosen, bright and elegant garnishes. Texture changes in the dishes will also keep alive your guests' interest in the food. And to keep up your own spirit, it almost goes without saying in this book that you should not choose more than one dish which cannot be substantially prepared in advance.

Wines

A menu planned from the recipes within this book will bring automatic suggestions for suitable accompanying wines. These focus on types and areas rather than specific châteaux or vintages, as you will no doubt have your own favourites. The long-established ruling of serving dry white wines with fish and poultry and red wines with red meat is still a reliable tenet but I do like occasionally to step outside the safety margins, enjoying a claret with chicken or a light red wine with grilled salmon. I recognise, however, that the choice of wine is a subjective affair and never more so than in the matter of what is dry and what sweet. This listing is intended as a guide to the types of wines you might drink with a dish and is to be seen as a starting point for your own experimentation.

Getting the Room Ready

Atmosphere and table presentation are vital components in the orchestration of a dinner party. They form the overture to the food and as such are essential mood-makers. In this area of preparation I attach no little importance to flowers. Obviously not the great hoops of blooms soaring over vast tables in Edwardian and Victorian houses or the capacious bowls of scented pot-pourri positioned around the 17th-century baronial halls, which anyone who watched the television series for which I was culinary adviser—*Upstairs, Downstairs*; *The Duchess of Duke Street* and *By the Sword Divided*—will be familiar with. But rather, for modern arrangements, as a confirmed follower of David Hicks's arrangements, I use glass tanks, round, square or oblong, both vast and miniature, into which I like to mass flowers of one variety, giving blocks of colour, which can be placed strategically in sitting or dining room and can be given a star role by the careful positioning of a spotlight.

Candles, too, should be assembled in masses, not singly or just in pairs and not necessarily on the table but in groups of five or six cleverly placed in two or three different areas. Church candles are good, because of their high beeswax content. They never clash, they don't drip (unless there is a draught), they are long-lasting and somehow it never looks as though you're using up the candles from a previous occasion. I leave them in their sticks and sconces when not in use as I find even unlit ones give a feeling that a room is lived in. And I always observe two basic rules when using candles: the electric lighting in the dining area should not be brighter than elsewhere in the house and I *never* have candles on the table at lunch time.

Electric light should be kept to a minimum: a subtle wash from a downlighter here, a clever glow across a wall from an uplighter there. Picture lights, if you have them, and the clever use of low-voltage spots are perhaps the most useful lighting for giving that added glamour to a room. And if controlled by dimmers, the effects can be variously and subtly balanced.

In addition to the basic rules about table-setting I apply two of my own. For me the element of surprise is all-important, achieved, for example, by the addition of a single treasured piece to the table or by the arrangement of the napkins (which I prefer to be crisply-starched double damask). The use of the under-plate is my second personal requirement. It allows a blending of antique and modern pieces and can, in the choice of a highly-decorated under plate underneath a plain top plate, add a colour theme to the table setting without overwhelming the food. The under-plate will also, in addition to the chosen cloth, to be an extra protection for your table against the heat. And do, incidentally, warm up any plates and serving dishes which are destined to receive hot food. A quick rinse under the hot tap will suffice if time is short. Chilled foods, on the other hand, should not be served semi-frozen as this will kill the flavour pleasure in your guests.

Clearing Up

Finally, to deal with the onus of clearing up, which can be such a damper for the host/hostess at the end of a party (though I actually enjoy it), here is a *modus operandi* to make this task less burdensome.

Have ready:
- Abundant hot water—turn up the thermostat or switch on the immersion early.
- Detergent—a mild one.
- A strong bin bag and tie—to take waste food and other débris plus an extra strong one to hold bottles.
- An old tin—to receive safely cigarette-ends and ash. (This should be put outside before you retire.)
- Clear work surfaces—to accommodate the dirty china and glass.
- Washing-up machine and sink empty at the ready—if you don't have a double sink unit, then arrange to have a large plastic washing-up bowl to act as a rinsing sink.
- An empty container—to soak cutlery. This can be a bowl, pan or plastic tub. Fill it with scalding water and a squirt of detergent.
- Extra rolls of paper towels.

- Plastic food containers, cling film and food bags—for leftovers.
- Trays—to act as extra work surfaces as well as a means of segregating china, glass, cutlery, etc.

- When you clear up, follow this sequence:
  Table → tray → work surface → soaking container → washing sink or dishwasher → rinsing sink → drainer → store cupboard.

When you wash, do:
- Wipe any plates which have mayonnaise on them with paper towels and wash separately. Mayonnaise is the kiss of death to washing-up water: it leaves a thin film of grease on everything.
- Segregate dirty china, glass and cutlery.
- Stack pans and bakeware, filled with soapy water where necessary, somewhere safely out of the way until you are ready to tackle them.
- Wash all glass first in hot soapy water and rinse in *hot* water.
- Scrape débris into débris container.
- Put cutlery into cutlery rinse before stacking plates ready for washing.
- Grade china in sizes.
- Empty, rinse out and re-fill the sink regularly.
- Drain well before drying.
- Stack, and line things up in an orderly fashion.
- Put a drop of washing-up liquid in scalding hot rinsing water.
- Lay a tea towel over the draining surface when washing glass: this protects delicate rims.
- Take off rings and other jewellery when washing up.
- Have a tea-towel impregnated with silver cleaner for that final buff-up.
- Stack for putting away, in the same orderly fashion as for clearing.

And don't:
- Stack glasses inside each other.
- Carry piles of plates with food and cutlery stacked between them.
- Fill your sink with a mixture of china, glass and cutlery.
- 'Push' china and glass against each other—this causes rims to be chipped.
- Wash glass in the same water as china and cutlery—this causes smearing.
- Hold a glass by the stem when drying it. Always 'cup' the glass in your hand and avoid any 'twisting' movement: dry 'one way'.

Herbs

Whilst in the late 1980s everyone should be planting fresh herbs, if not in their own special plot in the garden, then in window-boxes or in pots on the window-sill, it is not always practical to do so, and certainly it requires a deal of thought if you are to have a useful selection ready at the clip of the scissors. Yet herbs are accommodating, so, if I can persuade you to start a garden collection, then these are the ones you should grow: the ones most rewarding and most used.

- **Flat-leaf parsley (Hamburg parsley)**: the curly variety is the one herb readily available in our shops.
- **Chives**: they thrive on being snipped at. They also make a good edge to a border.
- **French tarragon**
- **Dill weed**: this provides fronds first, then seeds to dry.
- **Fennel**: this makes an attractive decoration as well, for it grows tall.
- **Coriander leaves**: for the stout-hearted. The seeds are good in Indian dishes.
- **Lovage**: a bit sophisticated, but if you have room, it is well worth the effort.
- **Basil**: for all those tomato salads and for Salade Niçoise.
- **A small bay tree**
- **A small rosemary bush**
- **Thyme**: don't forget lemon thyme.
- **Green, golden and red sage**: you only will use the odd leaf, but it looks so pretty in the garden and the leaves stay in winter.
- **Golden marjoram or oregano**
- **Mints**: grow two or three varieties for using in salads and drinks. Apart from peppermint, try ginger mint, apple mint and spearmint.

Dried herbs are a good stand-by, particularly if, like me, you are not green-fingered nor adept with the hoe and trowel. They will, however, lose their efficacy after a year (or less) and, as with spices, are adversely affected by light. They should be stored in a dark place and replenished from time to time. In recipes use half as much of a dried herb as of fresh.

What *is* useful in a kitchen is a 'string' of bouquet garni sachets for popping into soups and stocks.

NEVER, NEVER USE DRIED PARSLEY. It tastes like old hay and will mar the flavour of an otherwise perfect dish.

Spices

Try to acquire two or even three peppermills. This will enable you to ring the changes both in the kitchen and at the table.

- **Different peppers:**
  Black peppercorns
  White peppercorns or even coriander seeds.
  Mixed aromatic peppercorns: seek out a delicatessen where you can purchase tubs of these. This is a very rewarding pepper for milling over things at table.
  Cayenne: the very hot one rarely used.
  Paprika: sweet and warm.
  Java pepper: usually sold cracked, this is very hot and flavoursome.

- **Other spices:**
  Nutmeg, ground
  Mace, ground: the outside shell of the nutmeg and lighter in flavour

Ginger, ground
Curry powder: you will need 1 mild, 1 hotter, depending on your tolerance
Cinnamon, ground and, in the winter, in stick form for popping into mulled drinks
Coriander, ground
Saffron: this comes as strands or in powder form in little folded wax sachets, expensive but very rewarding.

- **Mustards:**
  Dry mustard powder
  Mild French mustard
  Wholegrain mustard
  Colman's: be it tarragon, mint, horseradish or wholegrain, keep a pot of your favourite.

Other condiments

- **Vinegars:**
  Red and white wine vinegar
  Mature balsamic vinegar
  Fruit vinegars: do try these, but they are expensive and you can achieve a better result using fresh fruit juice, with white wine vinegar.

- **Oils**
  Best olive oil: expensive and, perhaps, best kept for salad dressing and home-made mayonnaise.

Soy or other nut oil: for the health-conscious—it is light and flavourless.

Corn Oil: this has no place in my kitchen cupboard!—the flavour to me is too dominant.

As with the fancy vinegars, unusual nut oils are an expensive luxury, but it has to be said that a little walnut, hazelnut or sesame oil does add a sophisticated tone to a light dressing, particularly in warm salads. Keep in a cool place as these oils go quickly rancid.

- Soy sauce
- Tabasco sauce

- Horseradish in brine
- Tomato purée: in tubes
- Vanilla pods or essences
- Stock cubes:
    chicken, beef and vegetable.

Pots and Pans

It is false economy to buy cheaply produced pans. If you can afford to invest in good-quality pans, then they will be in your kitchen for your lifetime. I know, because mine have been—well, for 35 years and more, which is no bad recommendation. A well-made pan or casserole will be made of (in order of efficacy):

- *Copper, tin-lined.* Like the professionals used to use (they use stainless-steel today). Copper *is* the best conductor of heat, but it has to be cleaned after every use. It also has to be tin-lined and this can be a problem as tinners are not readily found.
- *Stainless steel.* This is easy to look after but is not a good conductor of heat, so it must have a copper-clad base or an aluminium disc brazed on, and the body of the pan should be—for want of a better term—3-ply: that is, two layers of stainless-steel sandwiching a layer of aluminium or copper. Now, you can't *see* this, so you will have to rely on the manufacturer's and shop's honesty to tell you that this is how the pan is constructed.
- *Cast-iron, enamel-coated.* Pretty to look at, a reasonable conductor of heat, *but* it *is* heavy

and will break if dropped on a hard floor, having first broken your foot if it hits you.

It is not easy to clean, as a glance round most domestic kitchens will tell you, and it does stick and heat-spot—particularly the frying pan, as those of you who have ever tried to fry bacon and eggs will have found to your cost.

However, the enamel does have a low—less than 2%—porosity, so it is safe to clean (soak) the pans with a light solution of domestic bleach or, as I have done since its advent, a solution of bio-degradable washing powder. Mine are pristine!

- *Non-stick.* Well, first of all, *non-stick does not mean non-wash.* These pans must be meticulously washed and dried, or carbon elements will build up and the pan will very quickly lose its non-stick surface. Nor do non-stick pans like a high heat, which means they are not suitable for brisk frying.

A small non-stick pan is ideal—nay, a must—for milk, cream, scrambled eggs and the like. Keep it only for these jobs. Ignore the claims of the manufacturers that you can use metal tools safely, and use wooden or plastic spatulas and spoons.

• *Calphalon*. When buying Calphalon, be prepared to discover that these are not as non-stick as the manufacturers may lead you to believe, nor are they all that easy to clean.

• *Plastics*. Always look for THERMO-SETTING PLASTIC. This is the sort of rigid utensil that won't soften when hot things are poured in. Thermo-plastic softens and is unsafe to use with hot things. Shop assistants won't know what you're talking about, but persist for safety's sake.

What you will need

Most sets of pan and bowls do not offer enough differential in size to be really useful. The small pan is not small enough, and the big are not big enough. For the average single-person kitchen you will need:

• **Lidded pans**
  2 × small pans, 1–1½ pints (570–825 ml) (one of these to be non-stick with Silverstone coating)
  2 × medium pans, 4–6 pints (2.3–3.4 litres)
  1 × very large pan, 12–16 pints (7–9 litres)

• **Lidded casseroles, and baking dishes.** These can be enamelled metal, flame-proof porcelain, oven-proof pottery, glass or pyro-ceramic.
  Casseroles:
  1 × 2 pint (or 1 litre)
  1 × 4–5 pint (or 2.5 litres)
  1 × 8 pint (or 4.5 litres)
  Baking dishes: A selection of sizes, 9 inches wide × 11 inches long × 2 inches deep (23 × 28 × 5 cms)

Oven-proof ramekins, 3½ inches (9 cms) in diameter

• **Wok**

• **Frying pans.** These should be heavy-gauge metal with a ground base.
  1 × 7–8 inch (18–23 cm) for individual omelettes and pancakes. This can be non-stick.
  1 × 12 inch (30 cm) for frying larger quantities.
  1 × 10 inch (25 cm) sauté pan with lid will make a good alternative.

• **Colander.** 1 large stainless steel, aluminium, or thermo-setting plastic 10 inch (25 cm)

• **Sieves.**
  1 × 9–10 inch (22–25 cm) fine-mesh wire sieve

1 × 4 inch (10 cm) conical fine-mesh wire sieve

- **Bowls and basins.** These can be stainless steel (expensive but there for life), glass, china or thermo-setting plastic. A varied selection will be gathered over the years, but for starters:
3 × 1 pint (570 ml)
3 × 2 pints (approx. 1 litre)
2 × 4–6 pints (2.3–3.4 litres)
1 × 12 pints (7-litres) large mixing bowl
1 pudding basin 1½–2 pints (approx. 1 litre) size

- **Baking sheets and roasting tins.** These should come with your cooker. You might like to add:
Swiss roll tin, non-stick 14 × 9 × ¾ inches (35 × 23 × 2 cm)
Wire cooling tray, oblong
9 inch (23 cm) pie plate, of enamelled tin or glass

- **Wooden kitchen aids.**
Chopping board 16 × 10 inches (40 × 25 cms)
Pan stand (triangle)
Salt box
Peppermill(s) see p.14
Rolling pin
Assorted wooden spatulas, straight-edged

- **Metal kitchen aids.**
Swivel-blade potato peeler
Citrus fruit zester
Kitchen scissors

Garlic crusher
Fruit juice press
Multi-faceted stainless-steel grater
Apple corer
1 small 2 fl oz (50 ml) ladle
1 large 5–6 fl oz (150–175 ml) ladle
Slotted spoon
1 flexible wire balloon whisk, 6-inch (15 cm) balloons
1 small stainless steel whisk, 3-inch (10 cm) balloons
Kebab skewers
Set of 6 scone-cutters, fluted or plain
Melon baller
Rotary whisk
Multi-purpose thermometer
Mincer
Scales

- **Glass or plastic.**
Measuring jug, 1 pint (570 ml)
A variety of sizes of plastic containers, lidded
Assorted scrapers and spatulas

- **Cook's knives.** A large 8–9 inch (20–22 cm) bladed cook's knife is a vital piece of equipment in the kitchen. Choose it carefully as it will be in full working use all your life, performing a whole range of tasks from chopping and slicing to shredding and crushing.

  Select a good brand name—Victorinox, Kitchen Devil, David Mellor, Wusthof—stainless-steel knife with a good molybdenum content in the steel to prevent the blade chipping. The blade should be ground evenly from spine to edge and not just have a ¼ inch (.5 cm) stamped-out edge.

The wood or dishwasher-proof plastic handle **must** be riveted through its entire length for strength and long service. With a large cook's knife, try the handle for size and balance as you would with a tennis racket. It should fit your grip comfortably.

You will also need a 7 inch (18 cm) smaller knife and a 3–4 inch (7–10 cm) paring knife.

- **Palette knifes.** These should have flexible stainless-steel blades throughout their length and not just bend at their tip, and the handles should be riveted through as with the cook's knife.

1 × 8 inch (20 cm) blade
1 × 4 inch (10 cm) blade

- **Electrical equipment.**
Coffee-maker—your own choice
4-slice toaster (you can use just one side for smaller amounts)
Food processor, plus all the attachments
Electric kettle
Tin opener
Hand-held whisk
A home smoker is a gadget to be considered as we hurtle towards our very own fin-de-siècle and a more health-conscious diet. Chicken, game, fish and meats are quickly turned into something other when lightly smoked over mesquite, oak or apple woodchips.

Nibbles, Soups and Simple Starters

Contents

*T*he ubiquitous Twiglet, crisp and nut, serve well as nibbles with drinks before dinner: they are however the butt of many a comment. At the other extreme there are those elaborations produced by caterers at formal receptions where sardines lie dead in a shroud of jelly.

Here I have devised six simple savouries which will take almost no time or effort to prepare, and I suggest you select just one (or at most a couple) and make up a handsome plateful for guests to be enjoying whilst you dart in and out of the kitchen.

Of course, a bowl or two of the stand-by mentioned above can supplement your own efforts in this field.

Smoked Eel on Rye Bread

*R*ye bread is available sliced in squarish packs. These nibbles can be made in the morning as rye bread doesn't go soggy.

Ingredients

8–10-oz (225–275-gram) pack of smoked eel

1 packet light Danish rye bread

butter for spreading

juice ½ lemon

black pepper

*A*dvance preparation
(5–10 minutes)

- Loosen 3–4 bread slices, and spread these with butter.
- Squeeze over a few drops of lemon juice (or use one or other of the savoury butters on p.139).
- Grind over a little black pepper.
- Lay fillets of the smoked eel to cover the entire surface, trimming off any untidy bits.
- Cut each square into 6 small bite-size pieces. Use a non-serrated knife for cutting: a saw-toothed blade drags the nutty bits in the rye bread.
- Arrange on a doilyed platter.
- Cover with plastic film and refrigerate.

An Exotic Dip

*B*ottled Parmesan is too gritty for this recipe. Buy freshly grated cheese from your purveyor. It keeps almost indefinitely in the fridge.

Ingredients

1 small tin of artichoke hearts (*not* bottoms), drained

2 ozs (50 grams) freshly grated Parmesan cheese

1 heaped Tablespoon bland mayonnaise *or* 2 Tablespoons thick cream

squeeze lemon juice

milled pepper

Tabasco sauce

20

Advance preparation
(5 minutes)

- Squeeze the excess moisture out of the artichokes.
- Using a cook's knife, chop these well on a board, then scrape into a basin.
- Mix in all the cheese and the mayonnaise or cream.
- Season interestingly with lemon juice and pepper and 3–4 shakes of Tabasco sauce.
- Cover with plastic film and refrigerate.

Accompaniments

- Serve with sticklets of washed celery, leaves of endive, carrot sticks or just plain biscuits.

Endive Spears with Keta and Soured Cream

This is very simple to prepare and quick.

Ingredients

2 small but plump heads of white endive
1/8 teaspoon milled pepper
1/8 teaspoon salt
2 teaspoons lemon juice
1/4 pint (150 ml) tub soured cream
1-oz (25-gram) jar Keta (red salmon caviar), refrigerated

Advance preparation
(5 minutes)

- Trim the brown bits off the end of the endive. Peel off the leaves into a sink of cold water.
- Drain well, and pat off excess water with paper towels.
- Store until ready for use, refrigerated, in a plastic bag sealed with a twist tie.
- Stir the salt, pepper and lemon juice into the tub of cream. Scrape this into a small glass or china serving bowl. Cover with plastic film.
- Do not open the caviar until ready to serve.

Finishing touches

- Choose a small tray or flat serving dish which will just contain the jar of caviar, the bowl of cream and the spikes of endive. Pile together, green tips outwards.
- Put two stainless or plastic spoons at the side of the caviar and cream and encourage your guests to help themselves by spooning a blob of cream on to the wide end of their endive spear, and topping this with a modicum of caviar.
- Black lumpfish roe can be used as an economic version if Keta is not easily available.

Hot Spiced Chicken Livers with Gherkins on Sticks

Some of the preparation of this delicious nibble can be done the evening before.

Ingredients

12 chicken livers
2 Tablespoons olive oil *or* soy oil
1 Tablespoon dark soy sauce
1 Tablespoon Amontillado sherry *or* whisky
5–6 dashes Tabasco sauce

1 level teaspoon milled pepper
¼ teaspoon ground mace
24 cocktail gherkins
24 satay *or* cocktail sticks
more olive oil *or* soy oil for grilling

Advance preparation
(10 minutes)

- If you have bought the chicken livers frozen, defrost overnight in the bottom of your fridge.
- Defrosted or fresh, put them in a sieve and rinse them under cold running water. Drain and pat dry with paper towels. Trim off any yellow bits and any bit of tissue. Cut each liver in half.
- In a small bowl mix together the oil, soy sauce, sherry, Tabasco, pepper and mace. Add the livers and coat well with this marinade. Cover the bowl with plastic film and store, refrigerated, until ready to grill or fry them.

Last-minute cooking
(20–25 minutes)

- Pre-heat the grill and the grill pan for 10–15 minutes. Have ready a serving platter or a dinner plate lined with a doily or folded white paper napkin. Slide a gherkin, 1 inch (2.5 cm) down the tip of each satay or cocktail stick and lay them ready on a plate or stand them upright in a milk bottle.
- Line the grill pan with a piece of foil. Brush this all over lightly with olive or soy oil.
- Arrange the chicken livers on this (in two batches if necessary—this will depend on the size of your grill pan) letting any marinade adhere to them. Grill the livers under a fierce heat for 1–1½ minutes *on each side*, turning them. They should be flared and slightly charred at the edges, so, if they catch fire don't worry, the flames will subside if you draw the grill pan away from the heat source for a few seconds and then replace it.
- Spike each liver on to its stick and pile them on to the paper-lined plate.
- Serve hot or warm.

Salami on Mustard-Buttered Rye-Bread Fingers

*A*gain, a speedy one to prepare and, if needs must, can be done the evening before.

Ingredients

1 packet light Danish rye bread, Vollkornbröt *or* Pumpernickel

butter, at room temperature
mild French mustard *or* wholegrain mustard
24 thin slices salami of your choice.

Advance preparation
(10 minutes)

- Using a small palette knife, carefully separate 6 slices of the bread and lay them flat on a work surface.
- Dab over evenly and spread each slice first with ¼ teaspoon of mild French mustard; then liberally spread with butter.
- Pick any casing (skin) off the salami. Cut each slice in half giving you a straight edge.

Arrange these on each piece of bread, three down each side and two across the ends, overlapping where necessary to get a tidy fit. Fill in the middles if there's a gap.
- Using a cook's knife (a saw tooth will 'drag' the salami) cut in half lengthways, then cut each half into two or three pieces.
- Arrange in one layer on a doilyed plate or platter. Cover completely with plastic film until ready to serve.

Smoked Salmon
Pâté with Whisky

*T*his pâté can be made 2–3 days in advance, and stored in the fridge. It *can* be made with smoked salmon off-cuts (which are cheaper), but do avoid dark pieces of the fish which can be stringy.

Ingredients

4 ozs (100 grams) Scottish smoked salmon

2 ozs (50 grams) unsalted butter, at room temperature

2 ozs (50 grams) Philadelphia cream cheese, at room temperature

3–4 dashes Tabasco sauce

juice of ½ lemon

¼ teaspoon ground mace

1 Tablespoon whisky

Advance preparation
(10 minutes)

- Put all the ingredients into a blender, make a fine purée, stopping the machine from time to time to scrape the sides into the main body of the purée.
- Scrape the pâté into a suitable small glass or china bowl from which you can serve it. Cover with plastic film and store refrigerated.
- If possible take the bowl from the fridge a couple of hours before serving, so that the pâté is spreadable. Don't remove the plastic film until just before serving.

Accompaniments

- Serve with brown or wholemeal toast with or without extra butter.
- A small bowl of 6 extra lemon wedges (see p.134) and/or peppermill of black peppercorns can be offered for those who want to use these.

*A*lmost since time began, soup has appeared at most mealtimes in Britain and most of the other cold-climate countries. A tureen of robust, warming broth functions in so many different ways: it's easy to eat, and warms the belly, 'lining' it as many say ready to receive the onslaught of greater dishes. It is also economical, simple to prepare and above all else, filling and tasty.

As our recipes and regimens have become more refined, so have our soups. The food processor and liquidiser have made it possible to produce those fine-textured purées once only possible from the stoves of professional kitchens where youths pounded away in mortars and rubbed coarse textured foods through fine hair sieves.

The greater use of refrigeration means that delicious iced soups can be an everyday affair if you wish. No longer is your choice limited to Gazpacho or Vichyssoise, good though these are.

I suggest you consider easing your evening work-load by serving soup in cups from a tray in the sitting-room. It's a talking point and means that you can do those last-minute jobs without being missed.

If you choose to adopt this method, then swap those top-heavy soup spoons for dessertspoons and tuck a small paper napkin 'twixt cup and saucer to dab away any wayward drops.

Chilled Mushroom
Soup with Sherry

*T*his is a rich soup which can be made up to two days in advance and stored in the fridge, covered with plastic film.

Ingredients

1½ lbs (700 grams) field (dark) mushrooms
1 small onion
2 Tablespoons olive oil *or* soy oil
1 clove garlic
1 chicken stock cube
1 heaped teaspoon mild French mustard

1 level teaspoon ground mace
1 level teaspoon milled black pepper
3½ Tablespoons Amontillado sherry
1 pint (570 ml) cold water
1 level teaspoon salt
2–3 teaspoons (a good squeeze) lemon juice
½ pint (275 ml) single cream

*A*dvance preparation
(50 minutes)

- Wipe but do not peel the mushrooms. Trim off and discard the dirty stalk ends, retaining the bulk of the stalks. Cut the mushrooms into rough but even-sized pieces.
- Peel the onion and cut in half, lengthways. Slice each half across into 7 or 8 slices. Separate the slices.
- In a large, heavy-bottomed saucepan, heat the oil until lightly smoking.
- Add the onion and garlic to the pan and, over a medium heat, allow these to soften and acquire a golden-brown colour, stirring them round with a wooden spatula and watching for signs of

them browning too much at the edges.
- Add the mushrooms and mix in. Fry for 2–3 minutes, stirring from time to time.
- Crumble in the stock cube and add the mustard, mace and milled pepper. Stir in.
- Pour in the sherry and water.
- Bring everything in the pan to the boil. Lower the heat and simmer, lidded, for 10 minutes.
- Allow to cool for ½ hour, then pour the contents of the pan into a large sieve set over a large 6-pint (or 3-litre) basin.
- In a blender, make a fine purée of the mushroom débris left in the sieve, using a spoonful or two of the liquid to moisten things. Do this in manageable batches,

returning the purée as it is made into the *basin*.
- Add the salt. Add more to taste if you like.
- Add the lemon juice.
- Allow to cool completely.
- Stir in the cream, using a small balloon whisk.
- Cover the basin with plastic film and chill in the fridge till ready to serve.

☰ *F*inishing touches
- Stir before ladling into chilled soup cups. As with all creamy, chilled soups, use a dessertspoon to eat it with.

Chilled Curried Pea Soup

*T*his lightly-curried soup should be made with frozen petits pois, as the skins are more tender than larger peas and give a smoother-textured soup. As pea soup loses its bright colour if left for too long, it can be made on the morning of the dinner party, or days earlier and deep-frozen before adding the cream.

☰ Ingredients

1-lb (450-gram) packet frozen petits pois
1 Tablespoon olive oil *or* soy oil
1 heaped teaspoon mild curry powder
2 teaspoons caster sugar
1 clove garlic
1 chicken stock cube plus 1 pint (570 ml) cold water *or* prepared fresh chicken stock (see p.137)

salt and milled pepper
½ pint (275 ml) single cream

☰ Garnish

¼ pint (150 ml) soured cream *or* strained Greek yoghurt
2 ozs (50 grams) cooked petits pois (taken from above)
sweet paprika (optional)

☰ *A*dvance preparation
(45 minutes)
- Overnight, defrost the packet of peas in the fridge.

- In a medium-sized saucepan, heat the oil until well-warmed but *not* smoking.
- Sprinkle the curry powder over

the oil, and stir it in, letting it fry gently for ½ minute.
- Add the defrosted peas, stir well in.
- Add the sugar.
- Crush the garlic in the garlic press and scrape it straight into the mixture.
- Crumble in the stock cube.
- Pour the water in, and bring the contents of the pan to the boil.
- Lower the heat and simmer for 5–6 minutes until the peas are just tender. Cool quickly to get rid of the residual heat which discolours them, by standing the pan in a sink of cold water, and stirring it to speed up the cooling process.
- Strain the soup through a fine-meshed sieve into a large bowl.
- Retain 2 Tablespoons of peas for garnishing later.
- Spoon half the remaining peas from the sieve into a blender or food processor with a metal blade. Add a few spoonfuls of the liquid and blend to a fine purée.
- As you finish each batch, tip the blended liquid into the basin.

Proceed until all the peas are puréed.
- Add salt and pepper, a little at a time, and taste to see whether it is to your liking.
- If you are preparing this days ahead and are going to deep-freeze it, allow the mixture to cool, pour into a covered plastic container and deep-freeze.
- If you are making the soup the morning before, stir in the single cream now. Chill, covered with plastic film in the fridge.
- Chill the soup cups.

Finishing touches
- If you have deep-frozen your soup, allow it to defrost in the fridge overnight or during the day, then stir in the single cream which should be at fridge temperature.
- Ladle into the chilled soup cups.
- Add a teaspoon of soured cream or yoghurt on the top for guests to stir in themselves.
- Add one turn of the peppermill, or a smidgen of sweet paprika, over the surface of each cup of soup as an extra garnish.

Chilled Smoked Salmon
Soup with Chives and Tarragon

*T*his rich, luxurious soup is best served in small quantities. Offcuts are not a good idea, since they are often tough and grey in colour.

▤ Ingredients

10 ozs (275 grams) good quality fresh
   smoked salmon
¾ pint (425 ml) cold fish *or* chicken stock
   (see p.137) *or* 1 chicken stock cube
   and ¾ pint (425 ml) boiling water
2–4 dashes Tabasco sauce
juice ½ lemon, strained

1 teaspoon milled white peppercorns (not
   regular white pepper: this is too
   pungent)
¾ pint (425 ml) single cream

▤ Garnish (optional)

16–18 leaves fresh tarragon
1 small bundle of chives

▤ *A*dvance preparation
                    (20 minutes)
- If you have no fish stock, use
  chicken, *or* cold chicken stock
  made from crumbling the stock
  cube into the boiling water,
  stirring and allowing to cool for ¾
  hour, or make up the day before.
- Cut the salmon roughly into 5-cm
  (2-inch) pieces.
- In a blender or food processor
  fitted with a metal blade, make
  the salmon into a fine purée,
  working in batches, and adding
  spoonfuls of the cold stock to
  moisten the mixture.
- Add the tabasco, lemon juice and
  pepper as you go along.
- Scrape each batch into a large
  bowl as you do it.
- Stir in any remaining fish or

chicken stock.
- Using a balloon whisk, stir in the
  cream.
- Chill for at least 4 hours before
  serving, by covering the basin
  with plastic film and leaving in the
  fridge until needed.

▤ *L*ast-minute preparation
                    (10 minutes)
- If you are adding the herbs, chop
  the tarragon leaves to make 1
  level Tablespoonful.
- Snip the chives (see p.131) to
  make 1 heaped Tablespoonful.
- Mix the herbs into the chilled
  soup.

▤ *F*inishing touches
- Serve in chilled *teacups* and eat
  with a dessertspoon.

29

Cream of Potato Soup with Basil

*T*his has a true potato flavour reminiscent of a more robust soup of yesteryear, yet possesses an elegance of its own. It can be prepared a day in advance, except for the final additions of cream and garnish, and can be served hot or chilled.

Ingredients

- 1½ pints (825 ml) hot or cold chicken stock (see p.137) *or* 1½ chicken stock cubes and 1½ pints (825 ml) boiling water
- 1½ lbs (700 grams) potatoes
- 2 ozs (50 grams) butter
- 1 clove garlic
- 4 × 1-inch (2-cm) thick leeks (white parts only)
- ½ pint (275 ml) double cream
- 1 level teaspoon salt
- 1 level teaspoon milled white peppercorns (black mars this soup's colour)

Garnish for hot version

- 3 large potatoes cooked whole
- 2 Tablespoons torn fresh basil leaves (12–16 basil leaves)

Garnish for chilled version

- 2 Tablespoons torn fresh basil leaves (12–16 basil leaves)
- 2 heaped Tablespoons snipped parsley fronds (see p.132)
- 3 Tablespoons snipped chives (see p.131)

*A*dvance preparation
(45 minutes)

- Make some stock (see p.137) *or* crumble the stock cubes into boiling water.
- Peel the potatoes and cut into ½-inch (1-cm) dice.
- Peel the garlic clove and slice thinly.
- Slice the white part of the leeks into ½-inch (1-cm) rings.
- In a large saucepan, melt the butter over a low heat without letting it brown, and swirling the pan round to ensure even melting.
- Add the garlic and leeks and mix well together. Put the lid on and let the leeks soften over a lowish heat for 7–8 minutes, stirring a couple of times.
- Prepare the potato garnish, by scooping out potato balls from the cooked potatoes with a solferino spoon (like a small melon-baller).

- Add the diced potato and stock.
- Turn up the heat, bring to the boil.
- Lower the heat to a good simmer (the soup will bubble gently) and cook for 20 minutes—this time without the lid—until the potatoes are fallen.
- In a blender or food processor with a metal blade, blend in batches to a fine purée.
- Pour into a basin and allow to cool before covering with plastic film and storing in the fridge till needed.

*L*ast-minute cooking
(5 minutes)
- For the hot version, reheat the soup in a saucepan. Do not allow to boil. Turn the heat right down.
- Stir in the cream, using a balloon whisk. The soup should be the consistency of good pouring cream.
- Check that the seasoning is to your liking.

*F*inishing touches
- For the hot version, add the potato balls and basil just before ladling into soup cups or plates.
- For the chilled version, mix the chilled cream and the herb garnish in together, leaving the soup with a 'marbled' effect, and ladle into cups or plates.

Chilled Herb Garden Soup

*T*his soup can be prepared exactly as the cold version above, adding a different garnish when you stir in the cream. Leave the soup for 4 hours, refrigerated, to allow the herb scents to develop.

Garnish

1 Tablespoon very fresh flat-leaf *or* curly parsley, very finely chopped (p.132)
1 Tablespoon fresh apple mint *or* ordinary mint, finely chopped (p.132)
1 Tablespoon fennel fronds *or* chopped tarragon *or* torn basil (not all three)
1 Tablespoon freshly chopped chives (p.131)
1 Tablespoon freshly chopped borage

Tomato
and Plum Soup

*T*his is a bright red, fresh-tasting soup, which can be served piping hot or ice-cold and is suitable for summer or winter. Ripe peaches can be used instead of plums. It can be prepared well in advance (the soup up to 2 days ahead; the garnish on day of use).

Ingredients

1 lb (450 grams) tomatoes
1 lb (450 grams) red plums
1 medium-sized onion
2 Tablespoons olive oil *or* soy oil
½ pint (275 ml) fresh tomato juice
1 pint (570 ml) fresh chicken stock *or* made from 1 stock cube
1 sprig fresh thyme *or* 1 level teaspoon dried thyme *or* 1 bouquet garni sachet

2 level teaspoons caster sugar
salt to taste
1 level teaspoon milled pepper

Garnish

2 plums
1 rounded Tablespoon finely chopped parsley (p.132)
1 rounded Tablespoon finely snipped chives (p.131)

Advance preparation
(40 minutes)

- Skin, de-seed and chop the tomatoes. (See p.135.)
- Cut the plums in half following the line of their cleavage. Discard the stones.
- Chop the onion (see p.131). Scrape on to a plate till ready for use.
- In a 6-pint (or 3-litre) saucepan, warm the oil without letting it smoke.
- Add the chopped onion, stir this round and, over a medium heat,

soften this without allowing it to get coloured and stirring it round to avoid excessive browning at the edges. This will take about 5 minutes. The onions should be transparent and a pale golden colour.

- Add all the remaining ingredients to the saucepan. Bring to the boil and simmer without a lid for 12–15 minutes until the fruits are soft. Cool a little. Then pour in manageable batches into the liquidiser and blend to a fine purée, pouring each lot into a large bowl. Cool completely and store covered in fridge.

- For the garnish: snip the chives and chop the parsley. (See p.132.) Mix together and store in small covered container in fridge.
- Cut each of the two plums in half. Discard the stones. Stand each half face up. Cut lengthways into 5 or 6 strips, then crossways into dice. Store, covered, in fridge.

≣ *L*ast-minute cooking
(5 minutes)

- If you are serving this cold, it requires no further cooking; if hot, reheat gently in a saucepan for 5 minutes just before serving.

≣ *F*inishing touches

- Pour into a pretty tureen or serve in individual bowls.
- Mix the chives, parsley and diced plum garnish and sprinkle over.

Avgolemono

*M*y version of this Greek lemon and egg broth is simple and tasty as long as you select a good brand of tinned chicken consommé. It can be served either hot (in which case it must be prepared at the last minute) or cold (in which case it can be prepared up to a day in advance). The garnish can be prepared a day in advance and stored in the fridge.

≣ Ingredients

2 × 12-oz (350-ml) tins chicken consommé (preferably Marks & Spencer's or Baxter's)
1 large *or* 1½ small juicy lemons
2 small eggs
1 scant level teaspoon milled white *or* black pepper
no salt

≣ Garnish

1 heaped Tablespoon finely chopped parsley (see p.132)
1 small bunch chives (1-cm/½-inch diameter) (optional)

▤ Advance preparation
(15 minutes)

- Pour the consommé through a small strainer into a medium-sized, stainless steel or enamelled saucepan. (Aluminium will discolour the finished soup.) Either discard or eat any bits of chicken retained by the sieve. Refrigerate consommé till required.
- Squeeze and strain the lemon juice into a small container. Discard the lemon skins.
- Break the eggs into a small basin. Beat them well with a fork until they froth. Put to one side.
- Snip the parsley for the garnish very finely (see p.132).
- Snip the chives into small pieces on to a piece of kitchen paper (see p. 131).
- Put both parsley and chives into sealed plastic bags and store in the fridge until required.
- If you are serving this soup cold, you can continue to prepare the soup in advance by following the instructions under 'Last-minute cooking', where relevant. The soup should be chilled in a covered basin in the fridge for 4–6 hours before serving.

▤ Last-minute cooking
(5 minutes)

- Have the consommé at the ready in a saucepan.
- For the hot version, have ready and warming in the oven at the lowest temperature 6 soup cups *or* large tea-cups. Have their base saucers ready in place on a tray.
- Have ready the egg and lemon and garnish in their separate containers.
- Mill the pepper on to a small square of paper. (To do this over the saucepan clogs the mill.)
- Bring the consommé to a rolling boil. This will only take 2 minutes or so. Turn off the heat. Leave for 10 seconds.
- Using a balloon whisk, briskly whisk in first the lemon juice and milled pepper.
- Whisk in the beaten egg, using a circular figure-of-eight motion with the whisk. Continue whisking for 8–10 seconds. You will raise a little froth. This is O.K.
- For the hot version, stir in the parsley and chives. (For the cold version, do not put the herbs in until you have cooled the soup in a basin and are ready to put it into the fridge.

▤ Finishing touches

- Ideally the soup should have the consistency of light cream. However, sometimes it curdles because of the imbalance of acidity. This in no way impairs the soup—in fact it looks quite attractive—but the soup should not be returned to the heat.
- For the hot version, ladle into the warmed soup cups and serve immediately.
- For the cold version, serve in chilled cups.

*J*ust when the word 'starter' crept into common use I don't recall. It does however cover the subject admirably well. Dishes can be hot or cold, liquid—as in soup or juice—solid or semi-solid. At one time we relied on the French Hors d'Oeuvre. However, thanks to the professionals, this took on the grim prospect of a trolley or side-table laden with *raviers* of tinned foods from baked beans to beetroot; an over-boiled egg-half or tired sardines lying in a pool of oil, being the highlight of the selection.

Happily today things are different as we eat more healthily and are becoming more inventive in the home.

Many dishes in this book have two places. Main courses, particularly the pasta ones, become starters when served in half-portions, and on a hot summer's day there is no reason why a sophisticated Boeuf Tartare should not fit the bill as an exotic main dish if you add a simple green salad to things.

If you feel that tackling a recipe is going to upset your equilibrium, go for the simple. Melon *is* ideal; it is *not* a cop-out unless you offer mean slivers of an unripe fruit. A half Ogen or Charentais melon makes a luscious starter. Likewise a dinner plate piled with curls of freshly cut smoked salmon is still a luxury and takes the pressure off you, as well as giving style to your dinner party. By the way, a half-lemon, wrapped in a piece of gauze—offered with either of the above—will earn you far more stars than a cut slice. Reserve that for the G.&T. with the slice and ice!

Simple Cold Red Pepper Salad

Straight from Italy! It can be a bother to prepare though it can be done several days in advance and refrigerated. When you are buying the peppers, don't buy those which are knobbly or have deep channels: smoother ones will make life easier when you come to skin them.

Ingredients

6 red bell peppers, approx. 2 lb
    (900 grams) in all
1 medium-sized onion
2 plump cloves garlic
6 Tablespoons virgin olive oil

1 teaspoon caster sugar
1 sachet ground saffron (optional)
salt and milled black pepper

Garnish

1 lemon, cut into wedges (see p.134)

Advance preparation
(50 minutes–1 hour)

- If you are using an electric cooker, pre-heat the oven for 20 minutes to 475°F or 240°C. Stand the peppers directly on the oven shelf and roast for 20 minutes until they blister all over.
- Remove and place in a plastic bag and tie it close, so that the steam will help loosen the skin. Keep them there for 5 minutes, then rub them through the bag.
- If you are using gas, pierce each stem with a cook's fork and hold the pepper over a high naked flame, turning as each section becomes seared and charred until they are black and blistered all over (about 4 minutes each). Put them into a bag as above, and rub them.
- Remove them from the bag and, under a cold tap, rub and rinse

36

all the skin away.
- Cut each pepper in half lengthways (from stalk to tip). Rinse out all the seeds under cold running water, and remove any white pith with a small, sharp, pointed knife, and discard. Pat each dry with a paper towel. Cut each half pepper into half again and then into ½-inch (1-cm) strips.
- Remove the onion's outer skin. Cut the onion lengthwise in half, then into quarters, then into eighths. Separate the layers.
- Peel the garlic and slice thinly.
- In a large frying pan heat the oil until just smoking.
- Add the onions and garlic, lower the heat, toss and turn the onion frequently until transparent and a pale gold.
- Add the peppers and fry till soft.
- Season with salt and pepper; sprinkle with sugar, and add the sachet of ground saffron for a more original flavour.
- Leave to cool, then store covered in the fridge until needed.

Finishing touches
- Arrange on small individual dishes with a wedge of lemon.

Accompaniments
- Serve with crisp rolls and a glass of dry white or red wine.

Potted Prawns

*P*otted foods are about as English a dish as you will find and one of the oldest ways of preserving foods. Potted Prawns make an ideal starter, and can be prepared a day or so beforehand.

Ingredients

1 lb (450 grams) frozen or vacuum-pack small peeled prawns
8 ozs (225 grams) good butter

½ teaspoons ground mace
½ teaspoon ground nutmeg
smidgin of cayenne pepper
salt sparingly

Advance preparation
(45 minutes)
- Boil some water in a small saucepan, cut the butter into pieces and add this to the gently boiling water.
- Allow the butter to dissolve completely. It will rise to the surface.
- Draw the saucepan to the side and

allow to cool. Put in the fridge to set the butter hard.

- Lift off the set butter, scrape clean, and pat the underside dry with paper kitchen towels.
- Put half of this clarified butter into a large frying-pan and heat it evenly until it foams and starts to go 'quiet'. Now add the mace, nutmeg and cayenne pepper and stir them in.
- Add the prawns and toss to coat them all evenly with the spicy butter. Don't add salt until you have tested them as they can be salty enough.
- Spoon into waxed cartons or 2½-inch (6-cm) wide ramekins and press them down. Allow to cool.
- Melt the rest of the clarified butter without letting it get hot and pour this over the top of the prawns to seal them.
- Store covered in the fridge.

≡ *Accompaniments*
- Serve with brown toast and chilled sparkling white Loire or Burgundy.

Boeuf Tartare

*T*his deceptively simple and rich dish makes a sophisticated starter. Ideal before any of the main courses: particularly fish.

≡ Ingredients

¾ lb (350 grams) fillet steak, free of all sinew, fat and skin, minced finely by the butcher

≡ Dressing

1 heaped teaspoon capers, drained
1½–2-ozs (40–50 grams) tin anchovy fillets and their oil
1 heaped teaspoon French mustard
2 egg yolks (see p.129)
1 heaped Tablespoon parsley, finely chopped (see p.132)
juice of 1 small lemon, strained
abundant pepper and salt
6 Tablespoons virgin olive oil (no other oil is good enough for this)

≡ Garnishes

6 lemon wedges (1 large or 2 small lemons)
1 heaped Tablespoon chopped parsley
a few capers
1 bunch watercress, washed and drained
9–12 slices brown toast halved

≣Advance preparation
(30 minutes)

- The minced meat, which should only be bought on the day you will use it, should be kept airtight and refrigerated until ready to mix at the last moment. This will prevent discoloration.
- An hour before the meal, you can prepare the following: put 6 8-inch (20-cm) or larger plates in the fridge to cool.
- Place the anchovy fillets and capers on a board, chop and mix them together with a cook's knife, leaving a coarsish texture. Transfer them to a bowl.
- Mix in the mustard, egg yolks, anchovy oil, chopped parsley (see p.132), lemon juice, salt, and pepper. Mix in the olive oil.
- Refrigerate, covered with plastic film, for 1 hour.

≣Finishing touches

- Just before serving, well mix the dressing with the chilled minced steak, using a dinner fork.
- Divide between the 6 chilled plates and press out into ¼-inch (.5-cm) thick circles.
- Sprinkle with a little extra snipped parsley, a few capers, add a wedge of lemon and sprig of watercress.

≣Accompaniments

- Serve with crusted slices of dry brown toast on to which each guest can pile a mouthful as they progress, or eat it with a fork, whichever is their pleasure.
- Pass lemon wedges, a small jug of olive oil, the salt and pepper mills for those who like their tartare oilier or sharper.
- Accompany with a glass or two of young Beaujolais.

*T*he high proportion of prawns to pasta gives this easy-to-prepare dish a luxuriant look. Shells are best as each holds a modicum of the dressing. Shrimp, strips of smoked salmon, flaked smoked trout or even cooked, flaked smoked haddock can be substituted for the prawns. All the preparation can be done a day ahead of time.

Ingredients

4 ozs (100 grams) small conchiglie (pasta shells)—dry weight
12 ozs (350 grams) fresh, frozen *or* vacuum packed (these are excellent) prawns *or* shrimps
1 bunch plump spring onions
2 medium beefsteak tomatoes *or* 3 smaller ones
2 Tablespoons snipped parsley (see p.132)

6 watercress sprigs
12 washed frisée *or* lettuce leaves

Dressing

1 small clove garlic
1 teaspoon French mustard
4 Tablespoons olive oil *or* soy oil
1 Tablespoon squeezed lemon juice
1 level teaspoon salt
1 level teaspoon milled pepper

*A*dvance preparation
(1 hour)

- Bring to the boil a large saucepan of salted water (1 teaspoon of salt to 4 pints (2¼ litres) of water).
- Tip in the pasta shells and boil gently for 10–12 minutes, leaving them a little *al dente* (firm to the tooth).
- Tip them into a colander and rinse them under the cold tap until they are quite cold. Drain well, shaking the water out of the cavities.

- Pat the shells dry with paper towels.
- Put the shells into a plastic bag into which you have poured 1 Tablespoonful of olive oil to prevent them sticking together. Work the oil over the pasta with the fingers through the bag. Put in the fridge till required.
- If you are using frozen shellfish, take them out of the pack a day ahead, put them into a dish and let them thaw *slowly* in the bottom of the fridge. If, in cold weather,

they are recalcitrant, leave them out in the warm kitchen for an hour or so to start them off. Otherwise keep all shellfish refrigerated at all times until ready for use. And never pour either hot or cold water over frozen shellfish to speed up the defrosting process; not only does this destroy the texture, colour and flavour, it more readily leaves the fish open to developing bacteria.

- Trim the roots off the spring onions, and any brown bits. Cut the spring onions into 1-cm (½-inch) pieces, cutting on the diagonal for aesthetic reasons only. Boil a saucepan of lightly salted water and tip the cut onions into this for 10 *seconds* only. This brightens the green colour and eliminates the onions 'repeating' when eaten! Immediately rinse them in a sieve under the cold tap. Drain again. Pat dry with paper towels, wrap in plastic film and put in fridge.
- Skin, de-seed and dice the tomatoes as instructed on p.135.
- Wash the parsley under cold running water and snip it as on p.132.
- Peel and crush the garlic, and shake all the ingredients for the Dressing in a screw-topped jar until creamy and well-emulsified. Store in the fridge until required.

▤ *F*inishing touches
- On 6 individual plates lay a couple of lettuce or frisée leaves.
- In a large bowl mix together the conchiglie, prawns, spring onions, tomatoes, parsley and Dressing, with a slotted spoon, and serve on to the lettuce leaves.
- Top each serving with a sprig of watercress.

▤ *A*ccompaniments
- A white Chardonnay or any similar full-bodied white wine will go well with this.

Baked Eggs 'en Cocotte' with Smoked Salmon

*T*here is only one secret to this deliciously luxurious recipe and that is: always pre-heat the oven for the same length of time; have the shelf in the same place; pour the same amount of water around, and time them with a stopwatch or 'pinger', noting how long it takes to get them to your liking in your particular oven. Much of this dish can be prepared 2–3 hours beforehand.

Ingredients

8 ozs (225 grams) smoked salmon
6 large eggs
butter for greasing ramekins

a little single cream *or* top of a bottle of rich milk
milled pepper *or* a pinch or two of paprika
salt sparingly

*A*dvance preparation
(30 minutes)

- Butter 6 ramekins. These differ in size with each make; but try to find some that measure about 3½ inches (9 cms) across.
- Take a shallow *ovenproof* container just large enough to hold the 6 ramekins with 1 inch (2.5 cms) space between them. Cut a piece of foil large enough to lay on top of the ramekins, and butter one side of it.
- Cut strips of smoked salmon about ¾ inch (2 cm) deep to line the sides of each ramekin. Press into place.
- Mince, or chop with a stainless steel knife, the remaining bits and divide equally in the base of each ramekin.
- Carefully break each egg into a teacup (just in case you break the yolk of one) and slide it into the ramekin.
- Spoon a teaspoon or so of single cream over each one.
- Mill a little pepper over *or* add a pinch of paprika.
- Add a smidgin of salt. (Remember that smoked salmon is already salty.)
- Stand the ramekins in the tin, lay the buttered foil over the top, and refrigerate until you are ready to use them.
- 20 minutes before you start to cook, pre-heat the oven to Gas

Mark 7, Electricity 425°F or 220°C.

Last-minute cooking
(10–12 minutes)
- Boil the kettle and pour the boiling water around the ramekins in the tin to about half way up. This is called a *bain-marie*.
- Bake the eggs, second shelf down, for 7–8 minutes or until the whites are just set.
- While this is cooking, get ready 6 tea plates with a small doily on each near the stove.
- Also have ready near the stove a folded teacloth and a few layers of paper towel.
- Lift the ramekins out in their water bath on to the stove top. With a dry cloth lift each ramekin on to the paper towels to dry them before putting them on to the plates.

Accompaniments
- Serve with hot buttered toast, crackers or bread rolls alongside, and eat with a teaspoon.
- Miss out on the wine with this one. Smoked fish and eggs are difficult to pair off. If you must serve wine, then a full-bodied white wine will be your safest bet.

Parma Ham (Prosciutto) with Melon

*A*n old timer, but still a favourite starter with many people, not least because it's easy to prepare. The success of this combination will depend entirely on the quality of the prosciutto and the ripeness of the melon.

Ingredients

1 medium-sized ripe melon *or* 3 smaller ones

12 full slices prosciutto (Parma ham)
1 large juicy lemon *or* 3 small limes
peppermill

Advance preparation
(15 minutes)
- The best small melons to buy are Ogen, Gallia or Charentais.

Larger ones should be yellow- or green-skinned Honeydew or orange-fleshed Cantaloupe with their mottled beige skins.

- Buy the prosciutto a day in advance, but ask the assistant in the delicatessen to ensure that the rind has been taken off and that the essential pieces of waxed paper are placed between each slice; otherwise it will be impossible to separate them without tearing the flesh. Store the prosciutto wrapped, in the fridge, till directly before you need it.
- Prepare the melon the morning before. Stand the melon on a board or work surface, and using a long-bladed, serrated knife cut ½ inch (1 cm) off the top and bottom and discard. Stand the melon upright and cut in half, starting at the top.
- Using a dessertspoon or teaspoon, scoop out all the seeds and discard.
- Cut each half lengthwise into 3 even-sized wedges.
- Take each wedge and remove the skin by carefully cutting between it and the melon flesh, following closely the line of the flesh. Discard the skin.
- Now, lay a wedge on its side, and holding it in place with the palm of your hand (fingertips stretched up out of harm's way), cut three thinner wedges, starting from the thicker side. Continue with the rest.
- Place the cut pieces on a large plate, wrap and seal with plastic film and refrigerate till directly before you serve.

- Cut the lemon in exactly the same way as the melon: top, tail, cut in half lengthways, then cut each half into three wedges. Cut away any ridge of white pith at the edges and, if the lemon is very pippy, pick out the main ones with a cocktail stick.
- If you are using limes, cut in half only, *equatorwise* this time.
- Put lemon or limes on a plate covered with plastic film in the fridge till required.

▤ *F*inishing touches
- For an elegant appearance use 6 dinner plates or pudding plates. Side plates are too small.
- Arrange 3 melon slices down one half of the plate.
- Lift the slices of ham from the paper and allow each to fall 'casually', one in each quarter of the other half of the plate. Don't be tempted to flatten it. Aesthetically, things should not overlap the rim of the plate.
- Place a wedge of lemon or lime strategically between the ham and the melon.
- Alteratively, the lemon or lime juice can be squeezed and strained into a jug for guests to help themselves.

▤ *A*ccompaniments
- Pass the peppermill for guests to use at will.
- A full-bodied white Chardonnay goes particularly well with this.

Warm Salads,
Pasta and Rice

Contents

*E*ver since I first met the 'composite salad' whilst training on the Continent my life has never looked back. It is the most useful dish known to man!

We threw out, or let drop into oblivion, that wonderful gallimaufry of our own—the Solomongundy, where fruits and vegetables, salad leaves, nuts and meats were all tossed in a wild extravagance before being doused in lemon juice, oil and honey, and liberally scattered with herbs and flower petals.

The marriage of almost any items works, though conflicting flavours should be avoided, and those salads which at one time were blanketed in a deliciously rich mayonnaise work equally well when yoghurt is substituted.

Thanks to Nouvelle Cuisine, the *Salade Tiède* is here, where a hot, or warm, main element is set on top of mixed salad leaves together with the pan juices which might well have been made into a new-style dressing with the added splash of a fruit vinegar and a drop or two of one of the *nouvelle vague* nut oils.

Warm Duck Salad with Hazelnut Dressing

*F*or those who like crispy duck skin, this is an ideal recipe.

Ingredients

3 duck breasts

Salad

12 mange-touts
2 medium carrots
1 small head of radicchio (about 12
   leaves) *or* frisée
1 cooked beetroot
salt

Dressing

⅛ pint (275 ml) hazelnut oil

⅛ pint (275 ml) olive *or* soya oil
2 Tablespoons sherry vinegar
½ Tablespoon French grain mustard
½ teaspoon salt
½ teaspoon freshly milled pepper
2–3 dashes of Tabasco sauce

Garnish

2 ozs (50 grams) toasted hazelnuts
finely shredded zest 1 orange
1 red apple
lemon juice
8 sage leaves

*A*dvance preparation
(40 minutes)

- For the salad, top, tail, string and shred the mange-touts.
- Peel the carrots and cut them into 'julienne' strips, that is, strips about ⅛-inch (.25-cm) thick and 1 inch (2.5 cms) long.
- Finely shred the radicchio or frisée.
- Slice the beetroot and cut into julienne strips.
- Shake all the ingredients for the dressing together in a screw-top jar.
- For the garnish, roughly crush the hazelnuts.

- Boil some water in a saucepan and blanch the orange peel by immersing it for a minute or two. Drain, rinse, cool, drain again.
- Core the apple, quarter it and slice it, and toss it in lemon juice.
- Shred the sage leaves.
- All the ingredients can be refrigerated separately, covered in plastic film, until you need them.

*L*ast-minute cooking
(25–30 minutes)

- Turn the grill on to high heat. Grill the duck breasts 6 inches (15 cm) from the heat source for 3–4 minutes on each side—allow

a little longer on the skin side so that the fat is properly cooked.
- Slice the breasts into 'scallops'—cut diagonally, about ¼-inch (.5-cm) thick.
- Bring a medium-sized saucepan of salted water to the boil, and dip the mange-touts and carrots into this for just 10 seconds to bring up the colour. Drain.
- Mix with the radicchio or frisée and beetroot, toss in the dressing and divide between 6 plates.
- Add the slices of duck on top.

▓ *F*inishing touches
- Sprinkle with crushed hazelnuts and strands of orange peel, topped with slices of apple and shreds of fresh sage.

▓ *A*ccompaniments
- Serve with a fulsome claret or Burgundy.

Salade Frisée with Chicken, Bacon and Croûtons

I couldn't stop adding extras to what the French call Curate's Salad. Shiitake are decorative Chinese mushrooms. But you can substitute regular white button mushrooms, which can be used to equal effect. Apart from marinading the chicken and cooking the potatoes, this is all last-minute cooking.

▓ Ingredients

Marinade

¼ teaspoon mace
¼ teaspoon ground ginger
juice ½ orange
1 clove garlic, crushed
1 Tablespoon rich olive oil

▓ Salad

2 × 6–8 ozs (about 200 grams) raw chicken breasts

4 new potatoes
4 slices of white bread, crusted
a little butter *or* soya oil for frying
8 ozs (200 grams) smoked streaky bacon
2–3 ozs (50–75 grams) shiitake mushrooms, washed
1 small flat lettuce
1 head of Belgian (white) endive
½ small head of curly endive (frisée)
8 clusters of lamb's lettuce (corn salad)
3–4 Tablespoons Herb Dressing (see p.139)

(1 hour)
- In a bowl mix all the ingredients for the marinade together well.
- Skin the chicken and slice diagonally into ¼-inch (.5-cm) thick 'scallops'.
- Put the scallops into the marinade. Leave for 30 minutes.
- Boil the potatoes and allow to cool. Slice these.
- If you like use a small fluted cutter to cut the bread into decorative shapes.
- Use on the sliced potato in the same way.

≣*L*ast-minute cooking

(20 minutes)
- Fry the croûtons until crisp in the butter or soya oil.
- Rind the bacon and cut it into long strips and grill or fry them to your liking. If frying them, retain the pan juices for frying the chicken scallops.
- Wash the mushrooms and dry with kitchen paper.
- Grill or fry the mushrooms and chicken using their juices as a basting liquid.
- Prepare the Herb Dressing (p.139).
- Toss the salad leaves and potato in the Herb Dressing.
- Add the cooked ingredients, the croûtons and toss together well.

≣*A*ccompaniments
- Serve a good white or red wine.

Warm Salmon, with Green Vegetables and Mint

*T*his also makes a delicious, simple starter.

≣ Ingredients

2 × 12 ozs (350 grams) salmon steaks

≣ Salad

4 thin leeks *or* 8 fat spring onions
8 spears asparagus, cleaned
1 small head fennel
4 sticks celery
1 green apple
a little lemon juice
olive oil for greasing
salt

≣ Dressing

⅛ pint (60 ml) olive oil
⅛ pint (60 ml) soya oil
⅛ pint (60 ml) lemon juice
1 level teaspoon Mint Mustard
1 Tablespoon yoghurt
1 teaspoon sugar
1 small clove garlic, crushed
12–16 small mint leaves, some shredded
    for dressing, some whole for garnish
salt and freshly milled pepper

▤ *A*dvance preparation
(30 minutes)
- Cut each salmon steak into 2 'cutlets' and skin them, or ask your fishmonger to do this.
- Shake the dressing ingredients together in a screw-top jar.
- Cut the leeks or spring onions, and the asparagus into 1½-inch (4-cm) long pieces. Cut the asparagus in half lengthways.
- Cut the fennel in half lengthways, and then into ¹⁄₁₆-inch (.25-cm) thick shreds.
- Cut or shred the celery in the same way.
- Core the apple, slice it and toss it in lemon juice.

▤ *L*ast-minute cooking
(25 minutes)
- Put the apple into a bowl with the mixed dressing.
- Bring a large pan of salted water to a rapid boil. Tip in the asparagus, 15 seconds later the leeks, and 15 seconds later the fennel and celery. Leave for only *5 seconds*. Lift out and drain.
- Tip everything into the bowl containing the dressing and apple and toss well.
- Divide between 6 serving plates.
- Pre-heat the grill to very hot.
- Cut each of the salmon 'cutlets' into 4 long slivers. Brush with oil, season lightly and place on a piece of oiled foil. Grill the slivers under the very hot grill for about 1 minute on each side. Turn, using a palette knife brushed with oil. Squeeze a little lemon juice over them.

▤ *F*inishing touches
- Arrange 2–3 slivers of salmon on each serving and pour over any juices.
- Scatter with mint leaves.

▤ *A*ccompaniment
- Serve with a rich white Chardonnay, Traminer or Rhône.

Chicken Liver and Spinach Salad with Walnut Oil Dressing

Ingredients

¾ lb (350 grams) chicken livers
enough milk to cover livers
½ lb (225 grams) young spinach

2 Tablespoons walnut oil
2 Tablespoons olive oil
salt and freshly milled pepper
2 ozs (50 grams) crushed toasted walnuts
2 pickled walnuts, chopped (optional)
1 Tablespoon olive oil
1 Tablespoon butter

Dressing

2 Tablespoons sherry vinegar

Advance preparation
(10 minutes)

- Trim the chicken livers of all skin and tissue. Soak them overnight in milk. Drain and pat dry with paper towels.
- Wash the spinach leaves, and devein them. Pat dry with paper towels.

Last-minute cooking
(30 minutes)

- Roll up 3–4 spinach leaves together. Shred them finely with a knife.
- Mix the ingredients for the dressing together.
- Toss with the spinach in a large bowl to coat each strand lightly.
- Divide between 6 plates.
- Scatter with crushed toasted walnuts and a sprinkling of pickled walnuts to add piquancy.
- In a frying pan heat 1 Tablespoon olive oil with 1 Tablespoon butter. Swirl around until evenly mixed, foaming and smoking lightly. Quickly sear the livers on both sides and cook leaving them pink, turning and moving them around. This should take no more than 2–3 minutes.
- Remove the livers from the frying pan and slice each one on the diagonal into 3–4 slices. Arrange them on top of the salad and pour the pan juices over the top.

Accompaniments
- Serve with an Italian red or white wine.

Pasta and Rice

*P*asta has returned to Britain almost as a staple. I say returned for in medieval Britain, centuries before the common potato was introduced, a form of pasta was popular. Richard II at his court would have been no stranger to 'Macraws' and 18th-century cooks would turn out *'Maccaroni with permafant Cheefe to drefs'*.

*R*ice too was a popular dish in our land; the Pilau appearing as a 'Pillow' or 'Pullow' of rice in many a cookbook.

I find a pot of savoury rice invaluable when I'm busy. It is virtually indestructible and can be prepared days ahead.

Pasta Shells
with Chicken (Cold)

*T*his is an easy, attractive-looking dish which can be made the day before using left-over boiled chicken (see p.137).

Ingredients

6 ozs (150 grams) conchiglie (small pasta shells)—dry weight
8 ozs (225 grams) cooked chicken
4 'middle' blades celery
2 medium tomatoes

Dressing

1 clove garlic

⅓ pint (190 ml) olive oil
2 Tablespoons red wine vinegar
1 heaped teaspoon mild French mustard
1 level teaspoon salt
1 level teaspoon milled black pepper
1 level teaspoon caster sugar

Garnish

2 Tablespoons parsley, snipped (p.132)
1 large juicy lemon, cut into wedges

*A*dvance preparation
(45 minutes)

- Cook the pasta (see p.40).
- Remove any skin, fat and bones from the chicken and cut the lean meat into 1-inch (2-cm) strips.
- Wash the celery and dice finely.
- Skin, de-seed and chop the tomatoes as instructed on p.135.
- Mix the cooked pasta, chicken, celery and tomatoes in a large bowl.
- Store in the fridge, covered in plastic film.
- To make the Dressing, first skin the garlic clove and crush it in the garlic press.
- Put the crushed garlic with the olive oil, vinegar, mustard, salt, pepper and caster sugar in a screw-topped jar. Shake vigorously until well-emulsified.
- Refrigerate, until needed.

*F*inishing touches

- Just before serving, pour the dressing over the salad ingredients, and toss everything well together.
- Either transfer everything into a clean salad bowl, or divide it between 6 plates.
- Sprinkle each well with parsley.
- Slice the lemon into 6 wedges (see p.134) and add one to each plate, or serve in a separate dish for guests to pass round.

*A*ccompaniment

- Serve a Rosé or any dry white wine.

I have unashamedly taken the recipe I use for the traditional Italian *Vitello Tonnato* and used it as a dressing for cold linguine pasta. The dressing is made up of mayonnaise (you can either make it yourself or use a shop-bought version of it) and Tuna Purée. All the components can be made separately beforehand—the pasta and the mayonnaise up to 2 days before, the Tuna Purée and garnish prepared a day before. Linguine are like fine, flattened spaghetti.

Ingredients

12 ozs (350 grams) linguine—dry weight
salt to taste
1 Tablespoon olive oil
2–3 Tablespoons French Dressing
    (see p.138)

Tuna Cream Sauce

½ pint (300 ml) mayonnaise (see p.130)
    or bland commercial mayonnaise
1 × 7–8-oz (225-gram) tin of white
    tuna in oil (not brine)
½ × 2-oz (50-gram) tin anchovy fillets

⅓ pint (190 ml) olive oil
1 slightly mounded teaspoon *mild* French
    mustard
1 level teaspoon freshly milled white
    peppercorns *or* regular black pepper
a few capers
juice of ½ lemon, strained
no salt

Garnish

1 handful parsley (to yield 1 teacup
    snipped parsley)
1 heaped Tablespoon snipped chives
3 medium-sized ripe but firm tomatoes

*A*dvance preparation
                    (1 hour)
- First the linguine, which can be cooked 2 days beforehand. Cook in boiling water for 8 minutes, stirring from time to time. Add salt at end of cooking. Drain, rinse, drain again.
- When the linguine have cooled, place in a plastic bag with a

Tablespoonful of olive oil, shake around to prevent sticking, and place in fridge to store till required.

- Prepare the French Dressing as described on p.138 and store in a separate container in the fridge.
- For the mayonnaise, which can also be made 2 days ahead, see p.130.
- The sauce is a mixture of mayonnaise and a tuna purée, which can also be made a day ahead. Put the tuna, its oil and the olive oil, and the anchovy fillets and their oil, mustard, pepper and capers into a blender.
- Using the lemon juice as liquid to moisten the mixture, make a creamy purée of everything.
- With a wooden spatula, scrape this purée into a basin.
- Cover the basin with plastic film, and store in the fridge till required.
- For the garnish, follow the preparations for parsley given on p.132.

- Snip the chives as described on p.131.
- Skin, de-seed and roughly chop the tomatoes as described on p.135.
- Store each of these three ingredients separately in containers covered in plastic film in the fridge till required.

*F*inishing touches
- Just before you serve, mix the linguine with the mild French dressing and sprinkle with the chives and parsley. Toss together with the chopped tomatoes.
- Divide evenly on to 6 large plates, or serve in a salad bowl.
- Using a small balloon whisk, gradually spoon the mayonnaise into the Tuna purée mixture, and mix to a creamy consistency.
- Serve this rich tuna sauce in a separate bowl or sauce-boat.

*A*ccompaniment
- Serve with a full-bodied Italian wine.

Tagliatelle Bolognese

I like a rich sauce, richer than the Italian, somewhat lighter traditional version, so I use a lot of wine and I always use rump steak. Fat-free mince is also good. The quantity of tagliatelle here will serve the 6, but I have given quantities for 12 for the sauce, so that you can deep-freeze half for another time.

Ingredients

12 ozs (350 grams) tagliatelle—dry
weight

Sauce

12 ozs (350 grams) best stewing *or* rump
steak, free of all fat
2 ozs (50 grams) onion
3 Tablespoons olive oil
3 ozs (75 grams) tomato purée

1 oz (25 grams) flour
½ pint (275 ml) red wine
1 large garlic clove
½ pint (275 ml) stock made from 1 beef
stock cube and ½ pint (275 ml) boiling
water

Garnish

3–4 ozs (75–100 grams) freshly grated
Parmesan cheese

*A*dvance preparation
(15 minutes)
- Cut away all the fat and sinew
from the steak and discard. Cut
the steak into manageable pieces
for the mincer or food processor,
using the metal blade. Mince the
steak.
- Skin and chop the onion
(see p.131).
- Crush the garlic.
- Make up the stock from the cube
with ½ pint (275 ml) boiling water.

*P*re-dinner cooking
(1 hour)
- In a heavy-bottomed frying pan,
heat the olive oil to a medium
heat. Fry the onions till golden
brown, stirring them with a
wooden spatula to make sure they
don't burn at the edges.
- Gradually add the minced meat,
stirring well with the spatula over
a good heat until the meat
browns.
- Add the tomato purée, taking care
to work it in well and see that it
does not burn.

- Sprinkle the flour over and mix
well in.
- Over a low heat—and here is the
secret of a good brown
sauce—gradually allow a crust to
form on the bottom of the pan.
This should take about 10
minutes, but watch it carefully.
- Remove the mixture to a large
dinner plate.
- Turn up the heat again and pour
in the red wine. Using the wooden
spatula, work all this crust into a
sauce.
- When the bottom of the pan is
clear, put the meat back into the
winey sauce, add the garlic and
the stock and simmer for 30
minutes.
- About 15 minutes before the end
of cooking time for the sauce,
rapidly boil a large saucepan of
water.
- Ten minutes before the end of
cooking time, add the tagliatelle in
two or three batches, letting it
slide into the water in its own good
time as it softens.
- Lower the heat so that the pasta is

55

boiling gently. Cook for about 8 minutes, till it is 'al dente' (cooked but not soggy).
- Add salt to taste. Drain the water off through a colander.
- Serve immediately on to warm soup plates, serve the sauce separately.

- Allow the other half of the sauce to cool before deep-freezing.

▤ Accompaniments
- Serve with grated Parmesan cheese.
- Red Chianti or any other Italian wine will go well with this.

Semolina Gnocchi with Parmesan Cheese and Tomato Sauce

*F*or pasta lovers, gnocchi makes an interesting variation on a cheap theme, and can be used in small portions as a starter or as a robust main dish when economy prevails. There are three main types of gnocchi: potato, flour and this one here made from semolina.

All the preparation can be done the day before.

▤ Ingredients

7 ozs (200 grams) semolina
1¾ pints (1 litre) rich milk
1 level teaspoon grated nutmeg
salt
4 ozs (100 grams) freshly grated
   Parmesan cheese
3 ozs (75 grams) unsalted butter
2 large egg yolks (see p.129)

▤ Tomato Sauce

1 × 12-oz (350-gram) tin plum tomatoes
¼ pint (150 ml) tomato juice
1 teaspoon Muscovado sugar
1 level teaspoon ground thyme
1 level teaspoon ground bayleaf
5–6 dashes of Tabasco sauce
1 teaspoon mild, sweet paprika
salt and freshly milled black pepper

▤ Advance preparation
(1 hour)
- Have the semolina ready on a plate.
- In a large non-stick saucepan

bring the milk to the boil with the nutmeg and salt. Lower the heat so that the milk bubbles gently.
- Using a balloon whisk, 'rain' in the semolina a little at a time,

stirring well to keep the mixture smooth.

- Let the mixture cook over a low heat for 12–15 minutes. Use a wooden spatula to help you keep the bottom and sides of the pan well mixed and to eliminate burning. Remove the pan from the heat.
- Separate the egg yolks into a bowl.
- Add half the grated cheese, *1 oz (25 grams)* of the butter and the 2 egg yolks to the pan, beating each well in as you work.
- Dampen about a square foot (about 30-cm square) of work top.
- Tip the gnocchi mixture on to this. Wet one hand with cold water and press the mixture into a square shape about ½-inch (1-cm) thick. Leave to cool for 1 hour.
- Well butter a shallow ovenproof dish about 14 × 9 ins (35 × 23 cm) using about 1 oz (25 grams) of softened butter and a small pad of kitchen paper to do this.
- Using a plain or fluted scone-cutter (or drinking glass) no more than 2 inches (5 cms) across, cut out the mixture into discs, dipping the implement into cold water between each cut, and wiping the edge clean with kitchen paper if it starts to clog.
- Cut up the leftover bits of gnocchi into 1-inch (2–3-cm) bits and lay them in the bottom of the dish.
- Dot with half the remaining butter and sprinkle with a little of the cheese.
- Using a palette knife, lift the rounds of gnocchi and arrange

these, slightly overlapping, in the dish.
- Dot each round with a bit of butter, using it all up, and sprinkle over the remaining cheese.
- Cover the dish with plastic film and put it in the fridge until you are ready to bake it.
- The Tomato Sauce can also be made a day before. Press and rub the plum tomatoes and their juice through a fine wire-mesh sieve set over a bowl. Mix with all the remaining ingredients.
- Bring them to boil in a saucepan, lower the heat and simmer for 3–4 minutes. Allow to cool and put in a container covered in plastic film in the fridge till ready for use.

*L*ast-minute cooking
(20 minutes)

- Pre-heat the oven to Gas Mark 8, Electricity 450°F or 230°C.
- Remove the film from the gnocchi dish and bake the gnocchi near the top of the oven for 15–20 minutes until a golden-brown crust has formed.
- While this is cooking, gently reheat the Tomato Sauce.

*F*inishing touches

- Sprinkle the gnocchi with any remaining Parmesan cheese.

*A*ccompaniments

- Serve the Tomato Sauce in a separate bowl.
- Because the gnocchi have a cheese topping, a light red wine would be good to serve with them.

The Italians are often scant in their use of ragus and sauces. I'm not! I allow a generous amount of bacon here, more than in Italy. Not much of this very simple dish can be prepared beforehand, but the last-minute cooking takes very little time.

Ingredients

12 ozs (350 grams) spaghetti
12 rashers long-back bacon (i.e. streaky *and* lean)
3 large egg yolks (see p.129)
½ pint (275 ml) single cream
1 level teaspoon milled black pepper

salt (¼ teaspoon or less for the sauce; 1 teaspoon to cook the pasta)
2 ozs (50 grams) butter *or* 3 Tablespoons soy oil

Garnish

4 ozs (100 grams) freshly grated Parmesan cheese

Advance preparation
(15 minutes)

- Cut the rind off the bacon with a knife or kitchen scissors and discard.
- Cut the rashers in half. On a board, arrange the pieces in manageable piles of, say, 4. Using a sharp knife cut each pile lengthways into 2 or 3 strips, then across into dice.
- Store in fridge or set aside ready for frying.
- To separate the egg yolks see p.129.
- In a basin well mix the cream with the yolks, pepper and salt, using a small balloon whisk to do so. Set aside or refrigerate covered with

plastic film as a skin quickly forms if the kitchen is hot.

Last-minute cooking
(20 minutes)

- In a large saucepan, bring about 10 pints (about 5 litres) water to a rapid boil.
- Lower in the spaghetti in 2 or 3 batches, letting it slide into the water in its own good time as it softens.
- Lower the heat so that the pasta is boiling gently. Cook for 8–10 minutes. Only add the salt when the cooking time is complete.
- As soon as you have put the spaghetti on to boil, put 6 soup plates or large dinner plates to

warm at the lowest temperature in the oven.

- In a large, non-stick frying pan fry the bacon over a good heat until brown, crispish, but not brittle. Push the bacon around with a wooden spatula to ensure even cooking.
- Set aside left in the frying pan till the spaghetti finishes cooking.
- Have ready a colander standing in the sink. As soon as the spaghetti is *al dente* (cooked through but still firm), tip it into this and let it drain.
- Quickly wipe out the saucepan and replace it on the stove over a low heat.
- Scrape in the fried bacon and its fats. Add the butter or oil and let this melt and get hot, stirring it all around.
- Return half the spaghetti to the saucepan and, using 2 dinner forks, lift and mix this well in. It takes time and patience.
- Add the remaining spaghetti and continue to 'grab' the spaghetti right at the base of the saucepan and down each side, lifting up the whole mass 'in-and-up-and-high' above the saucepan, letting it fall back each time.
- When all is very hot, and well mixed in, *and your guests are at the ready*, pour over the egg and cream mixture, mixing this in, in exactly the same fashion as above. Ideally you should try to mix it all in before the egg mixture solidifies with the residual heat of the pasta, but this doesn't matter, it will taste as good if it thickens a bit too much.
- Turn off the heat.

☰ *F*inishing touches
- Take the dinner plates out of the oven one by one and stand one at a time at the edge of the pan, on the stove top. Using the same two forks, 'grab' a portion of the pasta and lift this up, out, over the edge of the saucepan and on to the plate! You'll learn to manoeuvre pasta.
- Alternatively, tip the whole lot on to a large warm dish and serve it at the table—again with two forks, which after many years and in a domestic situation, I have found are easier to use than a wooden spaghetti fork, or tongs or a wooden spoon which is hopeless.

☰ *A*ccompaniments
- Serve plenty of grated Parmesan cheese in a dish which can be passed around.
- Any good Italian wine, white or red, will be fine with this.

Versatile
Savoury Rice
with Chicken and Ginger

*H*ere are no fewer than three recipes in one, for this can make a cheap and cheerful main dish on its own, or you can combine it with Chicken and Ginger, or with prawns or shrimps as an optional extra.

Some basic preparation can be done the night or morning before.

Ingredients

Savoury Rice

½ pint (275 ml) long grain rice (measured to that line in a measuring jug, or using a ½-pint (275-ml) mug)

1½ pints (825 ml) chicken, meat *or* vegetable stock made up from 1½ stock cubes and 1½ pints (825 ml) boiling water

6 rashers streaky bacon

1 × 4 oz (100 gram) onion

1 clove garlic

4 blades celery

4 ozs (100 grams) white button mushrooms

2 ozs (50 grams) butter *or* 2 Tablespoons olive oil *or* soy oil

2 sachets saffron powder (optional)

2 more ozs (50 grams) butter

3 ozs (75 grams) grated Parmesan cheese

2 Tablespoons double cream

2 heaped Tablespoons finely snipped parsley (see p.132) or other green herb

6 ozs (175 grams) prawns or shrimps (optional)

Chicken and Ginger

2 small chicken breasts

1 Tablespoon olive oil *or* soy oil

1 Tablespoon soy sauce

1 heaped teaspoon grated fresh ginger *or* 1 level teaspoon ground ginger

scant ½ teaspoon salt and milled pepper

1 extra Tablespoon oil for frying

*A*dvance preparation
(30 minutes)
• Make up the stock from the stock cubes crumbled in boiling water. Leave to cool, then store in the fridge.

- Cut the rind off the bacon with a sharp knife or scissors. Then cut into dice.
- Skin the onion and chop it finely (see p.131).
- Skin the garlic and crush it in the garlic press.
- Wash and dice the celery.
- Wipe the mushrooms with a cloth, and slice them finely.
- In a large metal casserole with a lid over a good heat, melt the butter or heat the oil.
- Fry the bacon until brown but not dry.
- Add the onion, garlic, and celery.
- Lower the heat and fry, stirring with a wooden spatula from time to time, until soft and perhaps a light golden colour.
- Add the rice and fry this for a minute or two, stirring.
- Add the mushrooms and mix in.
- Season with salt and pepper and mix in.
- If you are going to use saffron, add it and stir it in.
- This completes the advance preparation for the Savoury Rice. If you are going to add Chicken and Ginger, you can prepare it a few hours beforehand as follows.

- Skin the chicken breasts and remove the bones and discard. Cut the meat into as thin strips as possible by cutting each breast in half lengthways, then cutting each half across on the diagonal (aesthetics again!).
- Mix the oil, soy sauce, ginger, salt and pepper in a bowl.
- Mix in the raw chicken strips.
- Heat the extra oil in a frying pan over a good heat.
- Scatter in the marinaded chicken pieces, using a wooden spatula to mix and stir it round as it fries quickly. Fry it for 2–3 minutes, when it will be just cooked. Cut a thick strip in half to test it. Leave to cool in the frying-pan.
- Snip the parsley (p.132) for the garnish. Cover and put in the fridge.

≡ Last-minute cooking
(25–30 minutes)
- Pre-heat the oven to Gas Mark 6, Electricity 400°F or 200°C.
- In a saucepan, bring the stock to a rolling boil. Then pour it over the rice mixture in the casserole and mix well in, making sure nothing is sticking to the base of the casserole.
- Bring the casserole to the boil on top of the cooker, put on the lid, and transfer it to the heated oven as near to the top as it will fit. Leave it, unmolested, for 25 minutes.
- When the time is up, remove the lid and you will see that the rice is loose-grained and has absorbed *all* the liquid and the bits of bacon and vegetables have all risen to the surface in one cushion. Stir this all in, using a dinner fork.
- If you are not quite ready, the rice can be kept hot by putting it back in the oven with its lid on at Gas Mark ½ or Electricity 250°F *or* 120°C, for up to ½ hour without spoiling the dish, though it might dry out a little.
- Just before serving, stir in the butter, Parmesan cheese, double

cream and parsley, so have all of these ingredients ready at the side of the stove with a fork for mixing in.

- This is a meal in itself, but if you are going to add the Chicken and Ginger mixture, reheat it quickly in the frying pan and mix it in, adding any of the pan juices.
- Alternatively you can mix in your

prawns or shrimps (cold). The heat of the rice mixture will be sufficient to warm them through without toughening them.

*A*ccompaniment
- When used as an economical main course, serve plenty of dryish white wine.

Fish Dishes

Contents

Surrounded, as we surely are, by the stuff, we eat precious little of it, with the major exception of fish and chips (and good ones are difficult to find these days as the Chinese take over the business with their dyed pappy batter, frozen fillets and corn oil) and smoked salmon for the well-heeled. Almost all our catch of lobsters, oysters and prime white fish goes straight to France. My considered reason for this is that (until quite recently) fish has not been mongered for us as we—the customers—would really like it. The sight of so much dead fish lying on a slab of marble, glassy eyes staring mournfully into space, is about as off-putting as things can get.

Since the cod war prices have soared and many think twice before buying something that isn't that great a thrill to them. To many, fish is full of bones, and so it is.

It is those fish with 'cross-bones' which cause the problems, and I feel that more thought on how to fillet commercially herrings, mackerel and the like is needed. Surely, if shrimps, prawns and scampi can be successfully shelled mechanically, then the odd mullet shouldn't offer too much difficulty to the boffin.

Fish is good for us and we know it. Yet we eschew cooking it.

May be my recipes here will help change your mind.

Seviche of Salmon With Citrus Fruits

Seviching was an eighteenth-century way of semi-preserving fish where it was stored, raw, in wine, oil and herbs, not only in Latin American countries where today's renaissance has emerged from, but here in Britain as well. It is a delicious, up-to-the-minute way of serving our king of fish—salmon—and should be prepared 6–8 hours in advance.

Ingredients

8–10-oz (225–275-gram) piece middle-cut salmon

1 level teaspoon caster sugar
1 level teaspoon salt
1 level teaspoon milled white pepper
1 heaped teaspoon grated fresh ginger root (buy one small but plump root)

Marinade

3½ Tablespoons light olive oil *or* soy oil
5 teaspoons white or red wine vinegar
strained juice 1 orange
strained juice ½ lemon
1 heaped teaspoon mild French mustard

Garnish

1 pink grapefruit
1 large navel orange
1 small bunch chives *or* 4 spring onions
1 Tablespoon parsley, finely chopped

Advance preparation
(30 minutes + 8 hours' marinating time)

- Ask your fishmonger to skin and fillet the salmon for you.
- Depending on its shape, cut the salmon into two long pieces, then slice each piece into as thin slivers as you can manage—about ¼-inch (.5-cm) thick and bite-size in area!

- Choose a shallow porcelain or glass dish and arrange the salmon pieces in approximately one layer. Cover with plastic film and refrigerate this whilst you prepare the marinade and fruit garnish.
- Have ready a clean 10–12-fl oz (300-ml) screw-top jar. Into this put, in this order: the oil, vinegar, juice and then all the remaining ingredients.

- Put on the top tightly, and shake vigorously until you have a creamy-looking emulsion.
- Pour this over the salmon pieces. Re-cover with plastic film and leave refrigerated for up to 8 hours.
- The garnish can be prepared a couple of hours beforehand. The grapefruit and orange have to be knife-peeled and segmented, or peeled and thinly sliced to remove the bitter pith. (See p.134.)
- Snip the chives (see p.131) or shred the spring onions.
- Finely chop the parsley (p.132).

≡ *F*inishing touches
- Distribute the segments of grapefruit and orange over the marinated fish, and keep chilled till ready to serve.
- Serve on chilled fish plates, and sprinkle with the chives or spring onions, and the parsley.

≡ *A*ccompaniment
- It is difficult to marry wines with dishes of high acidity, but, if you want to serve a wine, a glass of Brut Champagne will work.

Seafood, Melon, Celery and Cucumber Salad with Yoghurt and Chive Dressing

*T*his refreshing salad can be prepared an evening ahead.

Ingredients

12 ozs (300 grams) freshly peeled prawns (*or* frozen)

6–8 ozs (150–225 grams) middle piece, turbot, halibut *or* haddock

½ bay leaf

light dredging of salt and milled pepper

6 nice ribs celery

⅓ cucumber

¼ medium-sized Honeydew *or* Canteloupe melon

strained juice of ½ large juicy lemon *or* 1 whole small one

scant level teaspoon salt

1 level teaspoon milled pepper

2 level teaspoons caster sugar (optional)

4 Tablespoons single cream (approx. ¼ pint/150 ml)

2 heaped Tablespoons finely snipped chives (1 inch dia. (2.5 cm) bundle or 1 'tray')

Dressing

3 good Tablespoons strained Greek yoghurt

Garnish

12 assorted small salad leaves

*A*dvance preparation
(45 minutes)

- If frozen prawns are used, allow them to defrost overnight in their bag in the bottom of the refrigerator. If you 'force' them to thaw by heating or putting in a microwave, they will discolour and toughen.
- The fish can be cooked the morning or evening before. Choose a lidded pan just large enough to hold the piece of white fish. Brush the base with a little oil. Put in the fish. Just cover with water. Add the piece of bay leaf, salt and pepper, and a slice from the lemon. Put on a lid. Bring to the boil slowly. Allow the fish to simmer for 1 minute. Turn off the heat and leave to cool completely in the water. Using a draining spoon, lift the fish out on to a plate. Remove the skin and bone, using fingers or a fork. Carefully break into inch-size (2–3-cm) flakes. Cover with plastic film and refrigerate until ready for use.
- While the fish is cooling, pull off any excess 'strings' from the celery ribs. Trim the ends of any discoloured pieces and discard

these. Holding a knife on the slant, cut each rib into ¼-inch (.5-cm) wide strips, also cutting them at an angle of 45° (for aesthetic reasons only!).

- Bring a small pan of lightly salted water to a rolling boil. Have a fine-meshed sieve or colander ready in the sink. Tip in the cut celery and allow to boil for 30 seconds. Strain through the sieve.
- Run cold water over the celery until it is cold. Drain. Pat away excess moisture with a piece of paper towel. Put on one side or store, refrigerated, in a small plastic bag until ready for use.
- Peel the cucumber with a swivel-blade peeler. Cut it in half lengthways. Using a teaspoon, scoop out the seeds and pulp. Discard these. Cut each half in half again lengthways. Cut each of the 4 strips into ½-inch (1-cm) thick pieces as you did the celery.
- Cut the melon in half. Cut one half into half again. Wrap the half and the other quarter not to be used in plastic film for another use. Refrigerate these. Scoop out the seeds from the quarter being used, using a teaspoon. Discard these. Cut the piece in half, lengthways. Using a small pointed knife, cut between the skin and the flesh following the line of the skin. Discard the skin. Cut each length of melon into pieces roughly the same size as the vegetables. Store in the fridge until ready for use in a small plastic bag or in a bowl covered with plastic film.
- To make the dressing, spoon the

yoghurt into a pint-size basin. Using a small balloon whisk, mix in the salt, pepper, sugar and lemon juice. Whisk well until everything is dissolved. Stir in the single cream. Snip the chives (p.131) and stir them in.
- Store in the fridge, covered with plastic film, until ready to assemble the salad.

☰ Last-minute preparation (10 minutes)

- Mix the two fish, melon, celery and cucumber in a large bowl, using a draining spoon to do this, running the bowl of the spoon down the side contour of the bowl, across the bottom and up the other side. This movement prevents breaking the foodstuffs up, which a 'stirring' movement might well do.
- Spoon over all the dressing, and mix in to lightly coat each morsel using the above movement.

☰ Finishing touches

- Line a platter with assorted salad leaves. Spoon the fish salad into the centre, leaving it piled somewhat.
- If you are not intending to serve the salad immediately, cover the entire dish loosely with plastic film, but making sure the edges are sealed and refrigerate.
- An alternative way would be to divide the salad between 6 8-inch (20-cm) plates, nicely mounded and garnished with the salad leaves.

☰ Accompaniment

- Serve with a Muscadet, Vouvray or Riesling.

Pan-Fried Trout
with Buttered Almonds

*T*rout are delicately-flavoured, easy to cook, and cheap. Be generous and purchase good-sized fish. The somewhat odd marriage of the soft-textured fish with that of crisp flaked almonds is a classic not to be missed.

This dish takes little time to prepare and tastes best when freshly cooked, though the almonds can be prepared in advance and reheated, and the cooked trout can be kept warm in the oven for up to 30 minutes without spoiling.

Ingredients

6 × 10-oz (275-gram) fresh rainbow *or* brown trout
4 ozs (100 grams) flaked almonds
3 ozs (75 grams) butter
juice ½ lemon, strained

2 Tablespoons white flour
1 teaspoon salt
1 teaspoon milled pepper
6 sprigs thyme *or* 3 bay leaves
2 × 4 Tablespoons olive oil *or* soy oil
2 × 1 oz (25 grams) butter
2 Tablespoons snipped parsley

*A*dvance preparation
(15 minutes)

- Make sure the fishmonger guts the trout and takes off their heads, tails and dorsal fins.
- To prepare the almonds, have ready a metal kitchen tray or china meat dish on which to tip and spread the browned almonds. Fried almonds can actually burn in their own residual heat, so the moment they are ready, they must be spread out to cool.
- In a frying pan over a low heat melt the 3 ozs (75 grams) butter without browning it. Swirl the pan around to ensure even melting. As soon as the butter is melted, tip in all the almonds and mix them well in, using a slotted spoon, to mix and coat them with the butter. You will now require patience. Working slowly and carefully, over a just-lower-than-medium heat, gather the almonds together from the sides of the pan and spread them out again. Continue like this until they are lightly

crisped and a good-to-medium toffee colour.

- Pour in the lemon juice. Salt and pepper them lightly.
- Tip out and spread them on the tray.
- Snip the parsley as shown on p.132, and keep in a covered container in the fridge.
- To prepare the trout, first prepare the seasoned flour. Scatter the white flour on to a large dish or plastic tray. Evenly sprinkle over this 1 teaspoon of salt and the same of milled pepper.
- Rinse each trout under cold running water. Drain and pat dry with paper towels inside and out.
- Push a sprig of fresh thyme *or* ½ bay leaf into the belly of each trout.
- Roll each trout in the flour to coat evenly. Shake away the surplus flour and lay the coated fish on a piece of kitchen paper set on a tray.
- Proceed to cooking stage right away.

≡ *L*ast-minute cooking
(20 minutes)

- In a large frying pan, heat 4 Tablespoons oil and 1 oz (25 grams) butter, swirling the pan around to ensure even heating. The oil/butter mixture will foam and splutter somewhat. When this starts to subside and go 'quiet', and you can smell a delicious nutty aroma, keep swirling the pan or the fats will start to burn at the edges. Cook the fish 3 at a time. Start over a good

medium-to-high heat.

- Using a palette knife or fish slice and cook's fork to move and turn the fish about, let the first side fry for 2 minutes until lightly browned. Turn the fish over by sliding the palette knife under its length, supporting and holding the top of the fish with the tines of the fork held almost horizontal, i.e. without piercing the flesh.
- Fry the fish for a further 2 minutes on this side, then lower the heat and continue frying and turning the fish at regular 1-minute intervals for a further 5–6 minutes (10 minutes in all).
- To test if they are cooked through, press the fish at the thickest part with the forefinger: it should 'give' easily.
- Lift them on to a warm serving dish, whilst you fry the second batch in the same manner. Discard the residue fats as they will no doubt be over-brown and full of untidy specks.
- While the second batch is cooking, put the first batch in the oven to keep warm at Gas Mark ½, Electricity 250°F or 120°C, and in the same oven reheat the almonds in a metal tray or meat tin for 10 minutes.

≡ *F*inishing touches
- Scatter the trout with the almonds and any of their buttery juices. Sprinkle with the snipped parsley.

≡ *A*ccompaniment
- Why not try a Blush wine or Rosé with this?

Fresh Salmon,
Haddock and Parsley Pie

*I*n this recipe for Fish Pie the two fish are put in *raw*. It is my new and delicious way of making this traditional British dish. The potatoes, parsley and eggs can be prepared the day before.

Ingredients

1½ lbs (675 grams) haddock fillets
1½ lbs (675 grams) salmon tail piece
4 eggs
salt and pepper
a little lemon juice
1½ ozs (40 grams) butter for buttering
    dish

Topping

2 lbs (900 grams) old potatoes
1 teaspoon salt
¼ pint (150 ml) cream

2 ozs (50 grams) butter
1 teaspoon milled pepper
¼ teaspoon grated nutmeg *or* ground
    mace

Parsley Sauce

2 large bunches parsley (to make 2 packed
    Teacups snipped parsley)
3 ozs (75 grams) butter
1½ ozs (40 grams) flour
1 pint (570 ml) milk
¼ pint (150 ml) cream
salt

*A*dvance preparation
(30 minutes)

- Put the eggs into a saucepan of cold water. Bring them to the boil. Lower the heat so that the water just bubbles and doesn't rattle the eggs about, which will crack them. Cook them for 8 minutes from boiling point.
- Pour off the boiling water and cool the eggs down by running cold water over them for 15 minutes or so. Crack the shells as you cool them to release the gases

and eliminate a dark ring round the yolk. Shell the eggs, holding them under running cold water. Pat them dry. Store in a plastic bag in the fridge.
- Prepare the parsley as shown on p.132, and store in a plastic bag in the fridge.
- Peel the potatoes with a swivel-blade knife, cut them into approximately 2-inch (5-cm) even-sized pieces so that they cook evenly. Put them into a saucepan, cover with cold water,

add 1 teaspoonful of salt, bring to the boil, lower the heat and cook them, uncovered, for 15–20 minutes. Test them with a skewer for doneness, they should break open.

- Drain them in a colander. Rinse out the pan, return the potatoes putting on the lid and tossing them over a minimal heat to dry them out for a couple of minutes. Using a traditional potato masher, mash them well. (Don't be tempted to use a food processor or you will end up with a glutinous mess!)
- Add the cream and butter, beating and mashing this well in until the potatoes look creamy, but are not sloppy.
- Season as you go along with more salt if liked, and 1 level teaspoonful of milled pepper, and a little nutmeg or ground mace.
- You will find it easier, having mashed them, to change to using a large dinner fork or a balloon whisk for the beating.

≡ *P*re-dinner cooking

(1 hour)

- Pre-heat the oven to Gas Mark 6, Electricity 400°F or 200°C.
- Well-butter a deep ovenproof dish approx. 9 × 7 × 3½ inches (23 × 18 × 9 cm) deep, or larger, using a pad of kitchen paper and about 1½ ozs (40 grams) of butter to do this.
- Remove the skin and bones from the haddock and salmon.
- Cut the fish into 1-inch (2–3-cm) cubes or pieces, mix together and put into the dish—raw! Season lightly with salt, pepper and a few drops of lemon juice.
- To make the parsley sauce, use a 2-pint (1-litre) non-stick saucepan set *over a low heat* and melt the butter, swirling it around to prevent browning. Using a balloon whisk, stir in the flour and allow this 'roux' (which is what this mixture is called) to cook *without browning* for 2–3 minutes, stirring a few times.
- In a second pan, bring the milk and cream to the boil, watching that it doesn't boil over. When the roux is ready, gradually ladle, or pour in the milk, whisking after each addition. Bring the sauce to the boil, lower the heat and cook for 5–6 minutes, again stirring from time to time. Mix in the finely-chopped parsley.
- Quarter the eggs and lay them on top of the salmon.
- Pour the sauce over the fish and eggs whilst it is still hot.
- Spoon over the potatoes and 'fork' up attractively.
- Put the dish in the pre-heated oven for 35–40 minutes. The top will be crisply browned and the fish cooked in its sauce.

≡ *A*ccompaniment
- A white Rhône or white Beaujolais will go well with this.

Minted Fish Kebabs

*T*his dish is ideal for cooking outside too, though I prefer to cook inside and carry the food outside.

Ask your fishmonger to skin and fillet all the fish, or, if you are purchasing from a supermarket, select portions which are prepared, but *don't use frozen fish*. It is too soft for this method of cooking.

The fish needs to be marinated for 3–4 hours before cooking, so much of this dish can be prepared well beforehand.

Ingredients

1 lb (450 grams) monkfish tail
1 lb (450 grams) halibut
1 lb (350 grams) salmon tail
2 small onions (1-inch/2–3-cm in diameter)
6 medium-sized white button mushrooms
1 red pepper
24 mint leaves
6 large or 12 smaller brochette skewers *or* satay sticks

Marinade

8 Tablespoons olive oil, soy oil *or* mixed
3 Tablespoons lemon juice (1 juicy lemon)
1 clove garlic
1–2-inch (3–4-cm) piece of fresh ginger
1 level teaspoon salt
1 level teaspoon ground coriander
1 level teaspoon milled pepper
5–6 dashes Tabasco sauce

Advance preparation
(30 minutes + 4 hours)

- Cut the fish into 1½-inch (3–4-cm) cubes or pieces, whichever looks appropriate. You are aiming to have thick pieces of fish of the same size to spike on to your skewer, i.e. 12 chunks of each fish, i.e. 2 pieces of each type for each of your 6 guests.

- Skin the onions. Cut into quarters. Separate the 'leaves'.
- Wipe the mushrooms clean. Cut into halves.
- Cut the pepper in half, then into quarters, shake out the seeds. Cut away the stalk and pith ribs. Cut each quarter into 3 pieces yielding 12 pieces.
- Crush the garlic in a garlic press.

72

- Prepare the marinade by mixing all the ingredients for this in a large 8–10-pint (4–5-litre) glass or china bowl.
- Toss the cubes of fish and the vegetables in this. Cover with plastic film and leave, refrigerated, for 3–4 hours or longer.
- On a clean work surface make groups of the marinated items:
  - 12 chunks:
    - monkfish
    - salmon
    - halibut
  - 12 pieces red pepper
  - 24 onion leaves
  - 12 mushroom halves
  - 24 mint leaves, folded in half
- Oil 6 large or 12 small skewers. Spike on the items, alternating them at will, but putting as many mint leaves in and amongst. Push everything well together, leaving 2–3 inches (5–7 cm) at both ends of the skewer, and ensuring that the filled skewers will fit under your grill or on to your barbecue.
- Leave the kebabs refrigerated on a meat dish covered with plastic film until ready to grill them.

▤ *L*ast-minute cooking
(20 minutes)
- Pre-heat the grill to a fierce heat. Grill the kebabs, 3 inches (8 cm) away from the heat source, for 12–15 minutes, turning them at 2-minute intervals. They should be somewhat browned at the edges and moist inside, and just cooked.
- Dab and brush them with any spare marinade or extra oil during grilling.

▤ *A*ccompaniments
- Serve on a bed of 2 heaped Tablespoons of Savoury Rice (see p.60) on 6 warm dinner plates. Lay one or two kebabs on top, leaving guests to push the fish off with their own dinner or fish forks.
- Serve a commercial brand of Barbecue Sauce or Minted Raita separately.
- A dry Tokay or full-bodied Chardonnay will go well with this.

73

Simple Grilled Salmon Steaks with Herb Butter

You score everytime a simple grilled dish is served. For modern-day palates the salmon should be slightly underdone and pink to the bone, but this is a matter of taste. This is a last-minute operation but is very quick.

Ingredients

6 × 1–1½-inch (3–4-cm) thick salmon steaks taken from the middle of the fish

4 ozs (100 grams) chilled Mixed Herb

Butter (p.140)

1 Tablespoon olive oil and 2 Tablespoons soy oil, mixed

salt and milled pepper

strained juice ½ lemon

Advance preparation
(30 minutes)

- Prepare the Herb Butter (see p.140).
- Pre-heat the grill to its hottest. This can take up to 15 minutes, depending on your type of cooker. The chamber needs to be hot as well as the elements.
- Line the pan with a piece of oiled foil. (You may have found that the albumen from fish, chicken or meat sticks to aluminium grill trays, particularly new ones!)
- Rinse any stray scales off the steaks under cold running water. Pat the fish dry with paper towels. Keep it refrigerated on a tray covered with plastic film until you are quite ready to grill it.

Last-minute cooking
(8–10 minutes)

- Arrange the steaks in two rows—thick parts to the middle—on the oiled foil.
- Spoon a little oil to cover each steak. Season lightly with salt and pepper and grill them 3 inches (8 cm) away from the element to seal them, for a good 1–1½ minutes. There will be—or ought to be—much spluttering and smoke, but this is meant to be as the fats ignite and 'fight' with the steam from the fish. Keep an eye on them.
- As soon as they are a good brown, remove the grill pan to a flat surface to turn them, by sliding a fish slice or broad spatula right under each steak, supporting the top with a palette knife. Don't try using tongs, the flesh is too delicate.
- Spoon over a little more oil, add the dabs of butter and grill the second side for a minute or so

74

until it is a good appetising brown. Lower the heat to medium and continue grilling for 2–3 minutes before turning the steaks back to cook the first side for 2–3 minutes. This will take about 8 minutes *in toto* depending on the thickness of the steaks.

- If you like your salmon well done rather than pink-to-the-bone, then cook them for a minute or two longer on each side.
- To test if the salmon is cooked to your liking, press the steak gently but quite firmly at the thickest part—right where the vertebrae is. It should give, and start to break into a distinct natural flake.
- To keep the steaks hot, don't leave them under the grill! Lift them on to a serving dish and cover this with a big balloon of foil. Put the dish into the oven at Gas Mark ½, Electricity 250°F or 120°C.

*F*inishing touches
- Top each steak with the cold butter *just* before serving.

*A*ccompaniment
- For a change, why not have a red wine to accompany this, as it balances the oiliness of the salmon admirably?

Cold Poached Salmon Cutlets with Mayonnaise

You need only buy three salmon steaks, but ask your fishmonger to cut each one in half, lengthways.

Ingredients

3 large salmon steaks cut 2 inches (7–8 cms) thick from the middle of the fish
1 Tablespoon oil *or* ½ oz (15 grams) butter

Special Poaching Liquid

1½ pints (825 ml) cold water
strained juice of 1 lemon
3–4 sprigs parsley
2 sprigs thyme
20 white peppercorns *or* 12 black ones
1 level teaspoon salt
2 Tablespoons olive oil *or* soy oil

Mayonnaise

6 Tablespoons commercial mayonnaise
1 Tablespoon cream
1–2 teaspoons lemon juice

Garnish

1 lemon cut into 6 wedges
6 sprigs watercress

▤ Advance preparation
(50 minutes + 1 hour to cool)

- You can cut the steaks in half yourself, if your fishmonger won't. Use a serrated knife (not a saw-toothed one, as this will drag the flesh). Leave the bones in and the skin on.

  The stock can be prepared 2–3 days in advance, and the actual cooking takes very little time. The fish can be poached the day before.

- Bring all the ingredients for the stock to the boil in a stainless steel or enamel pan. (Aluminium will discolour them slightly—but this is not harmful, just less aesthetically pleasing.) Lower the heat and simmer for ½ hour. Cool completely and refrigerate till required.

- Using 1 Tablespoon oil or ½ oz (15 grams) of butter, grease the base of a shallow lidded pan, just large enough to contain the 6 salmon 'cutlets' in one layer. Put the fish in. *Just* cover with some of the cold stock.

- Cut a circle of greaseproof paper to fit the surface of the fish. Butter or oil this and lay over the surface of the fish. This collects any scum and also 'contains' the steamy heat.

- Bring to the boil over a medium to low heat, put on the lid and simmer for 2 minutes only. Turn off the heat and leave the fish to cool in the liquid completely. This can take up to an hour. Discard the paper.

- Carefully lift out the fish on to a meat dish. Take off the skin. Remove any bones. Wipe the top surface clean with a piece of dampened kitchen paper. Cover with plastic film and refrigerate.

- Deep-freeze the remaining stock, which can be used in soup (p.29).

▤ Finishing touches

- Arrange on a dish or on 6 plates (not on lettuce as this gets messy).

- Mix the mayonnaise with the single cream and enough lemon juice—or water if the mayonnaise is lemony enough—to a soft—not *thin*—flowing consistency. It should well coat the back of a spoon.

- Spoon this over each cutlet stem to stern. Add a sprig of watercress and a wedge of lemon.

▤ Accompaniments

- Serve with new potatoes and a tossed salad.

- Accompany with a white full-bodied Chardonnay; Traminer or a delicious but dry Gewurztraminer is absolutely ideal with salmon.

Meat and Poultry Dishes

Contents

I wonder if, in the area where you live, you have ever noticed a 'Q' sign outside your butcher's shop? If so, your luck is in. The 'Q' guild is a nationwide assembly—or guild—of individual butchers who are prepared to butcher joints in the way you would like them. Lamb cutlets and best-ends will be skinned and French-trimmed with 50% of the fat scraped from the bone and the tiresome chine bone removed for ease of grilling, cutting and eating; braising meat and mince will be totally fat-free and if you want all the fat cut from a pork chop—which I must say would be a pity—then they will do this for you.

The better food chain-shops also have prepared joints for you to choose from and are now offering beef which has been well hung, making it more flavoursome. Try seeking out the manager of the butchery department and asking him how long his meat has been hung: your interest will please him and also prompt him to look to his laurels in this area. Praise always brings a better result than complaint!

As with poultry, and for that matter fish, fresh meat is going to give you a better result than frozen, particularly for grilling or pan-frying: the ice crystals in frozen meats create steam which causes toughening when heat is applied to it.

Look for bright-coloured, well-marbled beef and

pink-fleshed lamb with 'crisp' white fat, and making friends with your butcher is still good advice, even if he stands behind a supermarket counter.

Pan-Fried Calves' Liver with Grilled Bacon and Herbs

If you are to serve liver this way, then calves' liver it has to be. Lambs' liver is second choice. Ox and pigs' liver are out! Use them for a robust dish of liver and onions.

Ingredients

12 thin slices calves' (*or* lambs') liver
6 full rashers of good bacon
2 ozs (50 grams) butter

2 Tablespoons olive oil *or* soy oil
salt and milled pepper
1 large lemon
1 heaped Tablespoon snipped parsley *or* chives (p.131)

Advance preparation
(15 minutes)

- Get your butcher to slice the liver into thin, but broad slivers: about ¼-inch (.5-cm) thick, but 3–3½ inches (7–8 cms) across.
- Many packets of bacon contain a lot of water and are extremely salty, making it difficult to grill or fry them without creating a lot of steam: so get to know your bacon and buy fresh home-cured whenever possible.
- Cut ½ inch (1 cm) off the top and bottom of the lemon. Cut it in half, then cut each half into 3 wedges. Arrange on a plate, cover with plastic film, refrigerate.
- Using kitchen scissors, cut the rind off the bacon and snip the edges at inch intervals and ½ inch (1 cm) deep (this helps to stop it curling up too much).
- Snip the parsley or chives (pp.131–2), put into a cup, cover with plastic film and refrigerate until ready for use. All these jobs can be done the morning or evening before.

≡ Last-minute cooking
(20–25 minutes)

- Line the grill pan with foil and pre-heat the grill for 10 minutes. Grill the bacon at the same time as you fry the liver.
- In a large heavy-bottomed frying pan set over a medium heat, heat half the oil with half the butter swirling the pan around to ensure even heating. The fats will foam and splutter a bit. As soon as they go 'quiet' and are starting to give off a delicious nutty aroma and are looking slightly 'beige', turn up the heat to full.
- Using your fingers or cook's tongs, lower in the slices of liver, cooking no more than 4 at a time. Put the front edge of each slice into the hot fats and lower the slice gently away from you, so that you don't splash your hands.
- Fry the liver briskly on the first side for about 1 minute, moving them around a little as you fry. Using a palette knife and cook's fork (or tongs), turn the slices and fry for 1 minute on the second side. (Longer if you like liver well done. Just how long it takes to cook to your liking will depend on how thick the liver is.)

- Lightly season the slices with a little salt and milled pepper.
- Lower the heat whilst you remove the slices to a warm serving dish. Remember to turn the bacon rashers as they are ready and remove these to the serving dish. Arrange the slices of liver in a row, slightly overlapping.
- Keep things warm in the oven at Gas ¼, Electricity 225°F or 110°C.
- Turn the heat back up to full, adding more of the oil and butter to the pan. Fry the second and third batches in the same way, seasoning them and adding them to the dish as they are cooked.

≡ Finishing touches

- The liver can be cooked just before you sit at table, keeping it warm in the oven. Pour the pan fats over the liver, sprinkle with the chives or parsley if used, and arrange the bacon rashers on top. Pass the lemon wedges separately.

≡ Accompaniments

- Serve with new potatoes.
- For wine a claret, Rhône wine or Italian red will all go well with this.

Braised Pork Chops with Red Cabbage, Apples, Italian Sausage and Raisins

This is a particularly delicious way of cooking pork chops, much of which can be prepared a day in advance.

Ingredients

6 × 1-inch (2–3-cm) thick pork chops
8 ozs (225 grams) onions
2½ lbs (1 kg approx.) red cabbage
3 Cox's apples
6 ozs (150 grams) 'dry' Italian or Spanish sausage, such as chorizo
4 ozs (100 grams) muscatel raisins *or* sultanas
1 heaped Tablespoon brown sugar
1 heaped teaspoon salt
1 teaspoon milled black pepper
1 Tablespoon redcurrant jelly
3½ Tablespoons red *or* white wine vinegar
2 × 1 Tablespoon olive oil *or* soy oil

Savoury Paste for the Chops

1 oz (25 grams) butter
1 teaspoon milled black pepper
1 teaspoon sweet paprika
1 teaspoon salt
1 teaspoon dry mustard powder
1 teaspoon dried ground thyme
1 clove garlic, crushed

*A*dvance preparation
(1 hour)

- *Choose chops without a kidney,* and ask your butcher to remove the chine bone (the awkward shaped bit) but leave in the long bone. Ask him to take off the skin.
- Using a pair of kitchen scissors, cut the fat through at 1-inch (2.5-cm) intervals.
- Wet the end of a rolling pin under the cold tap, and bash the fat hard to flatten it. Wet the pin under the tap again as necessary to prevent dragging the flesh. (You can also use a clean hammer for this.)
- Put all the ingredients for the paste on to a dinner plate or directly on to a clean work surface. Using a small palette knife, mix and squash all these to a smooth paste.
- Spread a little of this paste evenly over both sides of the 6 chops, put on to a plate, cover with plastic film, and refrigerate until needed.
- Skin the onions, cut in half or to a size that will fit the food processor.
- Using the food processor fitted with the slicing blade, slice first

the onions.

- Cut the cabbage into quarters. Discard any damaged leaves. Cut away the thick white 'root' and discard this. Trim and cut the four wedges so that they will fit into the processor. Slice the cabbage.
- Cut the apples in half, then into quarters. Cut out the core. Slice roughly.
- Take the skin off the sausage. Cut it into four thick slices lengthways. Cut the slices into strips of the same thickness. Gather two or three strips together and cut into same-size dice.
- Store all the above ingredients in separate containers covered with plastic film in the fridge till required.
- Heat a large heavy-bottomed frying pan over maximum heat. (Non-stick should not be used as most non-stick surfaces will not withstand the high heat needed.)
- When you feel the heat coming up to your face, pour in 1 Tablespoon olive or soy oil, and swirl it around to coat the base of the pan.
- Using a cook's fork and large palette knife, lift in 2 chops at a time and brown them for 1 minute on each side. Remove the chops to a large plate or dish whilst you fry the remaining four. If you attempt to fry more than 2 or 3 at a time, you lower the heat of the pan, the chops don't seal and brown, the juices run out and the meat toughens.
- Allow to cool, cover with plastic film and refrigerate.

▤ *P*re-dinner cooking
(2 hours)

- In a large, wide, lidded pan, heat the oil until lightly smoking. Add the onion, stir, lower the heat to medium and let them soften and acquire a golden-brown colour. You will notice that the onions at the edges will brown quicker than those in the middle, so keep stirring them with a wooden spatula from time to time.
- When the onion is soft, stir in the other ingredients, a little at a time, sprinkling with the salt, sugar and pepper as you go along:
    sliced red cabbage
    sliced apples
    diced chorizo
    raisins, and
    redcurrant jelly.
- Add 3 Tablespoons water and the vinegar. Mix all well together. You'll find a slotted spoon easier to use to do this than a spatula. Cover with a lid, bring to the boil. Lower the heat and simmer, lidded, for 1 hour, stirring every 10 minutes or so.
- Pre-heat the oven to Gas Mark 6, Electricity 400°F or 200°C.
- Arrange the chops on top of the cabbage in a casserole in a circle, the thick part over the thin part.
- Bake, lidded, for 1 hour, the last 15 minutes without the lid to brown the chops.

▤ *A*ccompaniments
- Serve with small jacketed potatoes.
- Drink beer, or Alsace wine or a dry white wine from the Loire.

Herb-roast Shoulder (or Leg) of Lamb with Saffron Gravy

*A*s Saffron is expensive, this is optional in the recipe. You can use turmeric to give a similar colour, but the flavour won't be so subtle and provocative.

Ingredients

3½–4½-lb (1.8–2.2-kg) shoulder *or* leg of lamb
3 cloves garlic
2 large sprigs rosemary *or* thyme *or* lavender
2 ozs (50 grams) butter
salt and pepper
good sprig of thyme *or* 1 level teaspoon ground thyme
1 large carrot
1 onion
1 tomato

Gravy

1 dessertspoon flour
5 fl ozs (150 ml) red wine
½ pint (275 ml) stock *or* use a stock cube plus ½ pint water
2 sachets of 'Zaffy' saffron powder *or* 1 teaspoon turmeric
salt and pepper if necessary

*A*dvance preparation
(10 minutes)

- Make 10 or 12 deep incisions in the fleshy part of the shoulder with a small sharp-pointed knife.
- Peel and thinly slice the garlic and slide a sliver into each hole.
- Push a small sprig of rosemary and/or thyme or lavender into alternate holes. (If you like a stronger flavour, then put in more.)
- Rub the skin with the butter, season well with salt, pepper and dried rubbed (or chopped fresh) thyme.
- Clean and slice the carrot. Peel and slice the onion.

Slice the tomato.
- Put a cushion of the vegetables in the bottom of a roasting tin and stand the lamb on this.

*P*re-dinner cooking
(1 hour–1 hour 15 minutes)

- Roast at Gas Mark 9, Electricity 240°C or 475°F, for 45 minutes to 1 hour, longer if you prefer lamb well done (in which case lower the temperature to Gas Mark 7, Electricity 220°C or 425°F, after 20 minutes) and continue roasting.
- Remove the joint to a warm dish and keep warm in the oven at Gas Mark ¼, Electricity 110°C or

225°F. Decant away all but 2 Tablespoons of the pan fats.
- Stir in the flour: let this fry over a low heat in the roasting tin.
- Pour over the wine and stock.
- Sprinkle in the saffron.
- Check the seasoning.
- Let the sauce bubble gently for 10 minutes. Strain, boil down to ½ pint (275 ml) to give strength to the sauce.

▤ Accompaniments
- Serve with Savoury Rice (p.60) and Tomato Salad (p.111).
- A wine such as fruity Zinfandel will act as a good foil to the aromatic saffron.

Braised Lamb with Fennel and Orange in a Mustard and Sour Cream Sauce

Cubes of succulent lamb marry well with crisp fennel leaves. The contrast of the tart sour cream and warming mustard makes a very late-twentieth-century dish.

Ask your butcher to bone out the leg and trim off the excess fat and sinew.

You can have all the ingredients prepared in advance, but this is best eaten freshly cooked.

▤ Ingredients
4½-lb (2-kg) leg of lamb, boned
4 Tablespoons olive oil *or* soy oil
2 heads fennel
1 small onion (2 ozs/50 grams)
1 large clove garlic
1 heaped Tablespoon white flour
½ bottle Chardonnay *or* other dry but full-bodied white wine
¼ pint (150 ml) orange juice
2 heaped teaspoons Colman's wholegrain *or* French mustard
1 teaspoon Java pepper *or* milled black pepper
1 teaspoon caster sugar
salt to taste
shredded zest ½ orange
¼ pint (150 ml) soured cream

▤ Garnish
2 oranges
1 bunch parsley to make 2 Tablespoons snipped

83

Pre-dinner cooking
(30 minutes)

- The night or morning before, trim all fat and discard. Cube the lamb into 1-inch (2–3-cm) cubes, cover with plastic film and refrigerate till needed, as you can for the following ingredients when you have prepared them.
- Trim the base off the fennel and any discoloured bits, wash them, and quarter them lengthways.
- Skin and chop the onion (see p.131).
- Skin and crush the garlic.
- Grate the zest of orange.
- Prepare the garnish: peel the oranges, and knife-segment them as described on p.134.
- Snip the parsley as described on p.132.

Advance preparation
(2 hours)

- In a large, heavy-bottomed, lidded pan or metal casserole, heat the oil and fry the lamb cubes over a good heat to brown them well on all sides. I suggest that you do this in 4 batches, removing the lamb to a side dish as you brown each batch.
- Next, brown the fennel on all sides and remove to another side dish.
- Brown the onion, sprinkle with flour, and let this brown over a medium heat.
- Add the garlic.

- Pour in the wine, and orange juice, and work this into a sauce, using a wooden spatula.
- Mix in the mustard, add pepper, a little salt, sugar and the grated zest.
- Return the lamb and fennel to the sauce, putting the fennel on top in one layer. It doesn't matter that the sauce does not cover the fennel, as it will cook in the steam.
- Bring to the boil. Cover with a lid. Lower the heat and cook at a gentle bubble for 1¼–1½ hours. Take the fennel out after the first ½ hour so that it remains crisp.
- Remove the lamb again to a side dish.
- Stir in the soured cream, whisk it into the sauce.
- Return the fennel and the lamb to the pan to heat through.

Finishing touches

- Scatter the (cold) orange segments and parsley over the stew and serve direct from the pan or casserole, or from a warmed tureen or dish.

Accompaniments

- You can serve this with rice, or potatoes, or linguine, or, for a change, pearl barley cooked in chicken stock (see instructions on the packet!).
- A red or dry white Bordeaux, or Burgundy, or Chianti: any of these would go well with this dish.

Pan-Fried Fillet Steaks with Savoury Butter

A good fillet steak is ever popular. Ring the changes using different savoury butters from your freezer (see p.139). This is a last-minute dish.

▤ Ingredients

6 × 6-oz (175-gram) fillet steaks
2 Tablespoons olive oil *or* soy oil
1 teaspoon salt
1 teaspoon milled black pepper, mixed
   with 1 level teaspoon dry mustard
   powder

Savoury Butter (p.139)
or

▤ Sherried Pan Juices

pan juices
1/4 teaspoon only (heaped tip of the
   spoon) white flour, mixed with 1/4
   teaspoon dry mustard
1/2 beef stock cube
1/8 pint (50 ml) water
1/8 pint (50 ml) (1 large sherry glass)
   Amontillado sherry
1/8 pint (50 ml) tomato juice

▤ *L*ast-minute cooking
(15 minutes)

- In a heavy-bottomed frying pan, heat the oil until well smoking.
- Sear the six steaks over a fierce heat for 1 minute on each side.
- Lower the heat to medium, and continue frying the steaks for a further 3–4 minutes, turning them at 1-minute intervals. Cook them longer (6–7 minutes) if you like them well-done.
- Towards the end of their cooking time, season them liberally with the salt, pepper and mustard powder.

▤ *F*inishing touches
- Serve immediately with a pat of cold savoury butter or the sherried juices, prepared as follows:
- Set the pan back over a high heat.

Scatter the modicum of flour/mustard over and crumble in the stock cube whilst scraping and stirring rapidly with a straight-edged wooden spatula. Fry this for a few seconds only, all the time over a high heat.
- Pour in all three liquids. There will be much hissing, steaming and bubbling. Stir this small amount of sauce rapidly until all is cohered. It will only take 1/2 minute.
- Strain a Tablespoonful over each steak.

▤ *A*ccompaniments
- Serve with baby new potatoes and a tossed salad.
- This is the time for a rich red Burgundy.

Stir-Fried Tender-Loin of Pork with Black Beans

*E*verything can be cut and left at the ready the day before for you to perform at the stove at the last minute. If you don't have a wok, a large frying pan will do.

Black bean or yellow bean paste can be bought at any good supermarket or deli.

Ingredients

2 large tender-loins of pork (1¾ lbs/800 grams in toto)
1 bunch plump spring onions
2-inch (5-cm) plump piece of fresh ginger
1 small red pepper
1 small green pepper
3 ozs (75 grams) cashew nuts

2 Tablespoons Amontillado sherry
2 Tablespoons soy sauce
2 Tablespoons cold water
1 slightly rounded teaspoon potato flour
salt, milled pepper to taste
1 level teaspoon ground mace
soy oil for frying
2 cloves garlic, skinned and sliced
2 Tablespoons black (*or* yellow) bean paste

*A*dvance preparation
(45 minutes)

- If you cannot persuade your butcher to trim the skin off the tender-loins, you'll have to do this yourself. Take a small sharp pointed knife. Trim any fat off the tender-loin. Starting at the centre of the loin, pierce the 'opaque-looking' skin and slide the knife blade under, horizontally. Using little cutting motions cut away the skin, if anything, pressing the blade slightly upwards away from the flesh and helping things along by pulling the loin with the left hand against the knife. Do this in small sections until all the skin is off, turning the loin as you finish each section.
- Changing to a serrated knife, cut each loin into slivers no thicker than a 50p piece.
- Put the meat to one side, covered with a plastic film and refrigerated.
- Trim the spring onions of their roots and tops but leaving on as much green as possible. Slice these diagonally into inch-size (2.5-cm) pieces. Cover with

plastic film and refrigerate.

- Peel the piece of ginger, cut it in half lengthways, slice each half into thin slivers. Cover with plastic film and refrigerate.
- Cut each pepper in half from stalk to stern. Shake out the seeds and discard these; using a small pointed knife, carefully cut away the white 'ribs' of pith and discard. Cut each half pepper into four strips. Cut the strips into ½-inch (1-cm) squares. Cover with plastic film and refrigerate.

≣ Last-minute cooking
(15 minutes)

- In a cup, mix together the sherry, soy, water and potato flour. Put to one side.
- In a wok, or large frying pan, heat 3 Tablespoons of soy oil to searing hot. Have a large plate ready at the side of the stove.
- Stir-fry the pork tender-loin in manageable batches (about 4 batches), transferring each batch to the side plate as it is cooked (about 2 minutes for each batch). There should be much spluttering and smoke as you do this. If you add too much meat at one go, it will reduce the temperature of the oil and the meat will not seal, it will 'stew', steam will be given off and the meat will toughen. Add a

little more oil as needed. Season each batch with a modicum of salt, pepper and mace just before you take it out of the wok or pan. Line up all the rest of the ingredients.

- Rinse out and dry the wok or pan. Add 2 Tablespoons soy oil. Heat until smoking. Toss in the garlic and ginger and stir-fry rapidly for 30 seconds.
- Add the peppers and fry these for ½–1 minute, tossing and turning them over a fierce heat.
- Gradually incorporate the tender-loin.
- Lastly add the spring onions and carry on stir-frying until they just wilt, working hard to keep everything tossing, turning and heating right through.
- Mix in the black bean paste.
- Re-stir the sherry mixture in the cup and pour over the contents in the pan dispersing it in as wide a way as possible.
- Bring everything to the boil, stirring. Serve as soon as the modest amount of sauce has thickened slightly.

≣ Accompaniments

- Serve with plain boiled rice.
- Drink lager with this, or why not try rice wine (Saké) for a change?

Steak, Kidney and Mushroom Pudding

*T*his is a light, buttery version of the traditional pudding, not completely encasing the filling: just giving it an 'upper crust'. If you cannot obtain button mushrooms or onions, use larger ones, quartered. Some of the preparation can be done the morning before. I suggest you save this one for a weekend when you have more time.

Ingredients

Filling

2 lbs (900 grams) best stewing steak, trimmed of all fat
½ lb (200 grams) veal *or* lamb's kidney
½ lb (200 grams) button mushrooms
12 button onions
3 ozs (75 grams) butter *or* soy oil for frying
2 Tablespoons white flour
1 teaspoon salt
1 clove garlic, halved
2 sprigs fresh thyme (optional)
freshly ground pepper

Crust

5 ozs (125 grams) self-raising flour
1 level teaspoon baking powder
1 level teaspoon salt
1 level teaspoon freshly milled *white* pepper
3 ozs (75 grams) cold, hard butter
1 Tablespoon finely chopped parsley
1 Tablespoon finely grated lemon rind
1 egg

Advance preparation
(1 hour 40 minutes)

- For the filling, cut the steak into 1 × ½-inch (2–3-cm × 1-cm) sticks.
- Skin and core the kidneys (i.e. cut away the white gristly bits). Cut them into ¼-inch (.5-cm) thick slices.
- Wipe the mushrooms with a cloth to remove any dirt.
- Skin the onions.
- Have by you a large metal, lidded casserole.
- In a frying pan heat 2 ozs (50 grams) butter or oil until lightly smoking.
- Add the onions and lightly brown them; remove to the casserole.
- Add the steak to the pan in small batches, removing each batch to the casserole when lightly

browned. Salt sparingly.

- Mix in the mushrooms with the steak and onions.
- In a separate pan, quickly seal the kidney slices in the remaining butter or oil, and add to the casserole.
- Add the garlic, thyme (optional), and a little pepper.
- Pour just enough cold water into the casserole to cover the mixture (about 7½ fl ozs/210 ml at most). Cover the casserole and simmer over a low heat for 1 hour, stirring from time to time. Allow it to cool. If you are making this the morning before, refrigerate.
- While cooking this, start preparing the crust: mix the flour and baking powder in a mixing bowl and season with 1 level teaspoon salt and a little white pepper.
- Grate the butter on the coarse side of the grater and gently rub the grated butter into the flour.
- Chop the parsley (see p.132). Grate the lemon rind, and mix both into the pastry mixture.
- Beat the egg with 2 Tablespoons cold water. Add to the mixture and mix to a soft dough. Cover and refrigerate.

≡ Pre-dinner cooking
(2½ hours)

- Take a 2½-pint (1.5-litre) basin which will fit your steamer or large saucepan. Using a slotted spoon, put the steak and kidney mixture into the basin to within 1 inch (2.5 cm) of the top. (Any spare can be reserved and reheated in a pan.) Boil the remaining gravy until reduced by two-thirds, cool again, then pour over the meat.
- Turn the dough out on to a floured surface. Flour your rolling-pin. Press or roll out the dough into a circle large enough to cover the rim of the basin.
- Fit the crust over the steak and kidney mixture in the basin.
- Cover with buttered greaseproof paper.
- Butter a large piece of foil. Make a series of pleats across the foil and carefully push these up into a dome to allow room for the crust to rise. Place this over the greaseproof paper and tie down.
- Place the basin inside your steamer or saucepan and top up the pan with boiling water. Steam the pudding at a good roll for 2 hours.

≡ Accompaniments

- Serve piping-hot wedges of crust with spoonfuls of the filling.
- Accompany this with creamed potatoes (see p.112).
- A lusty red wine from Australia or California will go well with this.

Spiced Beef Stew
with Prunes and Pecan Nuts

*T*here was a time, in medieval England, when meat or fish with fruits and spices was the norm in our 'pottages' and 'brewets'. Things have come full circle and such marriages are popular again. Much of this dish can be prepared in advance: the garnishes the day before, and the stew half a day ahead.

Ingredients

3 lbs (1.5 kg) rump steak in one thick piece
2 heaped Tablespoons white flour, mixed with
  1 heaped teaspoon cinnamon
  1 heaped teaspoon milled black pepper
  1 heaped teaspoon mild curry powder
  1 heaped teaspoon ground mace
  1 heaped teaspoon ground coriander
2 teaspoons salt
1/4 teaspoon cayenne pepper
6 Tablespoons olive oil for frying
1/2 bottle red wine
2 Tablespoons soy sauce
8 ozs (225 grams) whole button mushrooms
2 Tablespoons olive oil
2 plump cloves garlic
1 × 2-inch (5-cm) piece of fresh root ginger
8 ozs (225 grams) onions

Garnishes

24 giant 'ready-to-eat' prunes
3/4 pint (425 ml) boiling stock, made from a beef *or* chicken stock cube

4 ozs (100 grams) pecan nuts
1 Tablespoon olive oil
1 teaspoon salt
1 teaspoon cinnamon

Advance preparation
(45 minutes + overnight soaking)
- Prepare the garnishes first. Make up the stock in a jug and add the prunes. Leave to soak overnight.
- In a small frying pan, *warm* the oil, mix in the salt and cinnamon, stir in the pecan nuts and fry them over a low.heat until they are crisp. Take them from the pan with a slotted spoon, and drain them on kitchen paper. Set aside till ready for use.
- For the stew, have ready a large

metal lidded casserole
(12 pint/6 litre).

- Cut all the fat and skin off the rump steak, visually divide the steak into 3 or 4 long strips about 1½–2 inches (4–5 cms) broad, into cubes, and crossways. Cut this.
- Put the flour, cinnamon, pepper, curry powder, mace and coriander into a large plastic bag. Shake the cubes of meat into this, coating them completely.
- Wipe the mushrooms clean with a damp cloth.
- Crush the garlic in the garlic press.
- Peel the ginger and chop it into small dice.
- Skin the onion and chop it (see p.131).
- In a large frying pan, heat 3 Tablespoons of the olive oil, and brown the meat in this—in 3 batches—on all sides over a high heat, working and turning the meat using a straight-edged wooden spatula to do this.
- As each batch is browned, remove it to the casserole using a slotted spoon. Add a little more oil to the pan between batches.
- When you have fried all the meat, there should be a good brown crust on the bottom of the pan. Lower the heat, tip in the loose flour from the plastic bag, and work this in quickly, letting it take on some colour.
- Pour in the wine, then scrape and work into the sauce the brown residues on the bottom of the pan. Let this bubble and continue to scrape and

mix everything together.
- Pour in the stock from the prunes, and soy sauce: allow this to boil and bubble for a minute or two.
- Add the whole mushrooms and cook these in the sauce for a minute.
- Pour everything into the casserole.
- Wash out the frying pan. Return it to a medium heat and heat the second 2 Tablespoons of oil without it smoking.
- Add the garlic and ginger, stir this round and fry it gently.
- Add the onions, stir them in and fry these to a golden-brown. Turn the heat up somewhat to do this.
- Transfer all this to the casserole and mix in.

≣ Pre-dinner cooking
(1½ hours)
- Pre-heat the oven to Gas 5, Electricity 375°F or 190°C.
- Put a lid on the casserole and cook the stew for 1½ hours, when the meat will be tender, but test it for doneness. Five minutes before the end of the cooking time, stir in the prunes to heat them through.

≣ Finishing touches
- Transfer the stew to a nice tureen if you wish, or serve it from the casserole.
- Sprinkle the spiced pecans over just before serving.

≣ Accompaniments
- Serve with plain boiled noodles.
- A young Beaujolais or a Côtes du Rhône goes very well with this.

Boiled Gammon (Ham) with Parsley Sauce

*T*his is economical to do and makes a great change from red meat. It is also useful for eating cold with a salad the following day, or for making a good ham sandwich to take to the office. It is also very simple to prepare.

Ingredients

3½–4-lb (1.3–1.8-kg) piece of prime gammon (smoked *or* plain)
2 bouquets garnis sachets

1 good teaspoonful peppercorns (about 20)

Parsley Sauce (see p.133)

*P*re-dinner cooking

(2 hours)

- Choose a lidded pan which will just contain the piece of gammon, without too much space around it. Fold a piece of foil into four, giving a square on which to stand the gammon to prevent it sticking to the bottom of the pan.
- Stand the piece of gammon on this, skin side up, if it will fit that way with the lid on. Cover with cold water, bring it to the boil, discard this first water and rinse any scum away under the cold tap.
- Re-cover with cold water, add the two sachets of bouquet garni and the peppercorns. Bring things slowly to the boil. Adjust the heat so that you have a gentle, but constant boil.
- Cook the gammon for 2 hours, topping up with boiling water from the kettle as necessary.

- Remove the gammon from the pan. Clip away the strings with kitchen scissors. Using a sharp pointed knife, score the skin at inch (2.5-cm) intervals to remove it more easily. Slip the knife under the strips of skin and cut these off. Discard.
- Keep the ham warm in the oven, the dish covered completely with foil, or pop it back into the warm liquid away from the heat.
- While the ham is cooking, make the parsley sauce. (See p.133.)

*F*inishing touches

- Turn the ham upright. Serve it, carved in thin slices with some of the sauce.

*A*ccompaniments

- Serve with crisply cooked broad beans, tossed in butter.
- Spicy Alsatian wine goes well with ham, or a full-bodied white wine.

*F*or me chicken, and a butter-roast corn-fed one to boot, is at its best when stuffed and crisply roasted *whole*.

However ready-to-cook poultry joints are now available in every conceivable form: boned chicken and duck breasts being the most useful. Make sure, however, that the skin is still intact, particularly if you want to grill the pieces. Buy them fresh—frozen chicken portions tend to be on the dry side. A succulent chicken breast is—just that—succulent.

Select breasts with just the thin rib cage left in. Ask your butcher to chop away the back bone and breast bone. Aesthetically the joints will look better, and they will fit more easily under the grill. The reason for leaving the ribcage bones in is to prevent the meat from shrinking too much.

I sometimes use boneless breasts, in which case they have to be grilled under a fierce heat quickly or they soon become too dry.

Whether or not you leave the skin on is a dietary question. I prefer it left on, for its protects the breast meat from drying, and I also enjoy the taste of lightly charred chicken skin, when the sugars caramelize, giving an extra dimension to the dish.

Roast Chicken with Bread Sauce and Forcemeat Balls

*R*oast chicken is a simple classic dish. Savoury little forcemeat balls are ideal for serving with it, or the mixture can be used to stuff the chicken.

Ingredients

Roast chicken

4–5 lb (1.8 kg–2.3 kg) chicken
2 ozs (50 grams) butter
½ teaspoon powdered rosemary
3 Tablespoons olive oil
salt and freshly ground black pepper

Forcemeat balls

6 ozs (150 grams) white breadcrumbs
    made from 6 slices medium cut white
    bread, crusted
4 rashers streaky bacon, plain or smoked
2 ozs (50 grams) suet
1 oz (25 grams) butter
1 heaped teaspoon grated lemon zest

1 teacupful snipped parsley fronds
    (1 big bunch)
1 large egg
2 small sprigs fresh thyme to yield 2
    teaspoons rubbed leaves
½ teaspoon salt
1 teaspoon milled pepper
2 further ozs (50 grams) butter for frying
1 Tablespoon soy oil

Forcemeat ball coating

8 slices fine white bread, crusted
1 large egg
salt, pepper
flour for dredging

Bread Sauce (See p.133)

Advance preparation
(1 hour)

- The forcemeat balls can be prepared 6–8 hours in advance or even the night before.
- Make fine crumbs of the 6 bread slices and the 8 slices separately.
- Cut the rind off the bacon with kitchen scissors or a knife. Cut each rasher lengthways into 3 strips, and cut or snip the strips into ¼-inch (.5-cm) dice.
- In a non-stick frying pan, over a medium heat, fry the bacon until crispish (it should not be brittle and dry), using a wooden straight-edged spatula to stir it around. Put a piece of paper towel on a plate. Remove the bacon with a draining spoon

on to this. Allow to cool.

- Stand a grater on a plate and using the medium/coarse teeth, rasp off 1 heaped teaspoonful of the lemon zest turning the lemon as you 'bare' each section.
- In a mug, using a fork, beat the egg with 1 Tablespoon of cold water until frothy.
- Snip the parsley (see p.132).
- In a large mixing bowl, using a dinner fork, mix well together the 6 ozs (150 grams) breadcrumbs, suet, salt and pepper.
- Mix in the parsley, thyme, lemon and bacon.
- Pour over the beaten egg, and gather the mixture into a softish 'dough' or mass, sweeping the fork round the sides of the basin and into the middle to do this.
- So that they don't stick and for ease of handling, have ready a lightly floured dish or plate to receive the forcemeat balls as you make them. Lightly flour a work surface, tip out the mixture, flour your hands and lightly press and roll the mixture into an evenly thick 'tube', sprinkling a little more flour over if things get sticky.
- You can either use this mixture as it is to stuff the chicken, in which case, wrap with plastic film and refrigerate till needed. But if you are making the tastier fried balls, then continue:
- Cut the roll into 6 large or 12 smaller pieces. Form and roll into balls, then pat into cakes using only the lightest pressure to do this. Take a palette knife and lift them on to the floured dish.

- Spread the second batch of breadcrumbs on to a dinner plate.
- Beat the second egg, season it and pour on to another dinner plate.
- Dip and coat each of the 6 or 12 forcemeat balls *first* with beaten egg, then roll them in the breadcrumbs, patting and pressing the crumbs well in.
- Shake off the loose crumbs and discard. Cover with plastic film and refrigerate the forcemeat balls until ready for use.
- Prepare the Bread Sauce (see p.133) at the same time and refrigerate.

*P*re-dinner cooking
(1¾ hours)

- First prepare the chicken for roasting.
- Preheat the oven to Gas Mark 7, Electricity 425°F or 220°C.
- Into the butter blend the powdered rosemary and some salt and pepper. (You can do this by mashing it well with a fork on a plate.)
- Rub this mixture all over the skin of the chicken.
- If you are going to stuff it with the forcemeat, push the forcemeat into the flap of skin left where the neck was, and pin the edges of this to the chicken with a wooden skewer or cocktail stick.
- Stand the bird in a roasting tin, on a rack.
- Pour over the olive oil, put a piece of foil over the breasts to prevent scorching.
- Place in the oven on the middle shelf and cook for 1½ hours or until the thighs are tender but not

over-cooked. Baste frequently during the roasting time.

- Whilst the bird is roasting, reheat the bread sauce (see p.133).
- If you are frying the forcemeat balls, allow 15 minutes towards the end of the cooking time for the chicken to do this.
- In a frying pan over a medium heat, melt 2 ozs (50 grams) butter with 1 Tablespoon soy oil until lightly smoking, swirling the pan around to ensure even colouring and heat.
- Lift the balls into the pan using a palette knife to do this. Fry them for 1½ minutes on each side when they will be golden-brown and crisp. Keep warm in the oven or warming compartment until ready to serve them.

*F*inishing touches

- Remove the chicken to a warm serving dish. Take care to remove any string, and take off the wing-tips for easier carving. Place the fried forcemeat balls around the chicken.

*A*ccompaniments

- Serve with Jacket Potatoes (p.110), Bread Sauce and Minted Peas (p.110).
- Serve a light claret or white wine.

Baked Chicken Breasts with Spinach and Tomato in a Cheese Sauce

*M*arks and Spencer offer a good range of ready-made sauces. Cheese Sauce is one of them. Failing the availability of this, use one of the better makes of packet sauce.

Much of this dish can be prepared the day before.

Ingredients

6 × 8-oz (200-gram) chicken breasts
12-oz (350-gram) packet of frozen leaf spinach
3 × 3-inch (7.5-cm) diameter tomatoes
1 oz (25 grams) hard butter

¼ teaspoon ground mace
salt and milled pepper
½ lemon
1½ pints (825 ml) cheese sauce
4 ozs (100 grams) Gruyère cheese
2 ozs (50 grams) flaked almonds (optional)

≡ *A*dvance preparation
(30 minutes)

- Leave the spinach to defrost in the refrigerator overnight.
- Take it from the pack and put it in a colander in the sink with a plate with a heavy weight on top to press out all the liquid. Help things along by squeezing it dry with your hands.
- Well butter an 11 × 9 × 2-inch deep (28 × 23 × 5-cm deep) ovenproof dish, using a pad of kitchen paper and a walnut of butter.
- Sprinkle a good pinch of two of ground mace over the bottom of the buttered dish.
- Remove the stalks and cut out the 'eyes' of each tomato, and using a serrated knife cut each into 4 or 5 slices. Lay these over the bottom of the dish.
- Sprinkle lightly with ½ teaspoon of salt and a dredging of milled pepper.
- 'Disentangle' the spinach, fluffing it up with the fingers and cover the tomatoes with this. Season lightly with a little salt and pepper.
- Cut the piece of hard butter into 12 little cubes and disperse these evenly over the spinach.
- Skin and remove the bones from the chicken breasts.
- Take each breast and cut it into 4 thin slivers by holding a serrated knife at 45° and cutting on the diagonal in long slices.
- Use a palette knife to lift each group of slices on to the bed of spinach. Squeeze a few drops of lemon juice over the raw breasts and also season lightly.
- Make up the cheese sauce if you are using it from a packet.
- Spoon it over the breasts.
- Grate the cheese and sprinkle it over, mixed with the flaked almonds (if you are going to use them).
- Refrigerate till ready to use.

≡ *P*re-dinner cooking
(35 minutes)

- Pre-heat the oven to Gas Mark 6, Electricity 400°F or 200°C for 15 minutes.
- Stand the dish on a shelf above the middle of the oven and bake for 20 minutes.
- The dish will come to no harm if it has to be kept waiting for ½ an hour or so. Prop open or leave the oven door ajar, lowering the temperature to Gas Mark ½, Electricity 250°F or 120°C.
- Stand the dish on a platter to transport to the table.

≡ *A*ccompaniments
- Serve with Jacket Potatoes (p.110).
- White Burgundy or a light claret goes very well with this.

Grilled Chicken with Oriental Spices

*F*or the diet-conscious grilled chicken breasts are ideal. They're also easy on the pocket.

Ingredients

6 × 10-oz (275-gram) large fresh
   chicken breasts, bones in
olive *or* soy oil for grilling

Marinade

2-inch (5-cm) thick piece of fresh ginger to
   yield 2 teaspoonfuls grated

2 teaspoons salt (or less)
1 level teaspoon ground black pepper
1 level teaspoon ground mace
2 level teaspoons ground ginger
1 teaspoon Tabasco sauce
1 large clove garlic
2 Tablespoons soy sauce
½ teacup olive *or* soy oil

*A*dvance preparation
(30 minutes + 4–6 hours for marinating)

- The marinade can be prepared at least a day in advance.
- With a small knife or swivel-blade peeler, peel the ginger. On the coarse jagged-toothed side of the grater, grate the ginger on to a small plate (to catch the juices). The reason for the large piece is to make this job easier and protect your finger ends! Discard the peel and any nub of leftover ginger after grating.
- Scrape into a 6-pint (3-litre) glass, enamel, stainless steel or china bowl. Now using a small balloon whisk add: salt, pepper (milled first on to a piece of paper), mace, ground ginger, Tabasco.
- Crush the garlic and add.
- Mix to a paste with the soy sauce.
- Whisk in the oil.
- If you are preparing this a whole day before, cover with plastic film and refrigerate as the aromas will permeate anything nearby.
- You can at this time also prepare the chicken for marinating.
- On a wooden or plastic board or work surface (melamine slips!) take each breast in turn and lay it with the 'pointed end' vertically away from you.
- Pull and snip off the skin if you have decided not to use it.
- Using a serrated knife (not saw-toothed—this drags the flesh), make 4 × ½-inch (.5-cm) deep incisions across each breast, cutting diagonally from top left and across ending up ½-inch (1-cm) lower on the right-hand side of the breast. Cut each incision ½ to ¾ inch (1–2 cm) apart or thereabouts. This is to let the marinade do its job, and the heat from the grill to get into the thick part of the meat quickly.

- Arrange the breasts in one layer on a plastic tray or china meat dish (check that this will fit into your refrigerator).
- Cover with plastic film and refrigerate overnight if you have done this in advance, or until ready to add the marinade.
- 4–6 hours (or more) before grilling, remove the plastic film. Stir the marinade well and, using a tablespoon, spoon some over each breast, until used up.
- Re-cover with the plastic film, refrigerate.
- Turn the breasts at hourly intervals, 'trampling' them well in the marinade.

≣ *L*ast-minute cooking
(30 minutes)
- Pre-heat the grill to spanking (searing) hot. Leave the pan and rack under! This takes up to 15 minutes, as good grilling is best achieved when the entire grill chamber is very hot too. Have ready a little olive or soy oil and a brush.
- Remove the grill pan and brush the grill rack with oil.
- Using a pair of tongs lift each marinaded breast—allow any marinade to adhere—lay them flesh side up on the pan.
- The size of your grill will establish whether you grill the breasts 3 at a time, or all 6 together. They should be about ½-inch (1-cm) apart. Too many reduces the heat too quickly and they start to steam.
- Replace the grill pan under the heat 4 inches (10 cms) from the heat source. Let the chicken sear

and seal. There will be much spitting, spluttering and flaming too if you're doing the job properly: just let it happen.
- After 2 minutes or so, have a look and establish that the flesh is beginning to brown well. Turn the breasts over and allow the same to happen on the undersides. You can let them really sear and singe on this side as the rib cage bones will protect the flesh.
- Depending on how well done you prefer chicken, continue grilling them for 1 minute on each side until they have had 6–8 minutes *in toto*. Brush and dab them as you go along with any spare marinade.
- To test for doneness, pierce the thickest part of the flesh with a bodkin or skewer. Press the flesh with the forefinger. If the juices run bloody, then cook some more. If they are golden with only a modicum of pink, they're O.K.
- Remove them to a warm serving dish and serve when ready.
- If you want to do all this before your guests are seated at the table, do so, and keep them warm—uncovered—in the oven set at Gas Mark ½, Electricity 250°F or 120°C. If you keep them hot for more than 15 minutes or so, the juices will start to run, but this doesn't matter, and, anyway, you may prefer your chicken well done.

≣ *A*ccompaniments
- Serve with a really simple green salad and a jacket potato (p.110).
- Serve with lager or Saké.

Chicken Casserole
with Celery and Mushrooms
in a White Wine and Tomato Sauce

*A*ll the preparation for this simple and tasty dish can be done the day before.

Ingredients

3 large chicken breasts
6 thigh *or* leg joints
½ head celery
8 ozs (225 grams) mushrooms
4 ozs (100 grams) onion
2 × 400-gram tins chopped tomatoes in
   natural juices (Cirio)
½ bottle dry white wine
1 teaspoon mace, mixed with
   1 teaspoon salt
4 Tablespoons olive oil *or* soy oil
further 2 Tablespoon olive oil

1 clove garlic
2 heaped teaspoons white flour
1½ teaspoons salt (or less)
pepper
2 teaspoons caster sugar
2-inch (5-cm) piece of lemon rind
2 sprigs thyme

Garnish (optional)

1 bunch spring onions
1 heaped cup snipped parsley fronds
   (1 very big bunch)

*A*dvance preparation
(1¼ hours)

- Chop the wings off the chicken breasts and chop the breasts in half, making an oblique cut. Chop or cut away excess backbone. Chop the 'ankle' off the legs, and chop each leg through the drumstick joint. Trim the joints of excess fat and skin only.
- Wash the celery and cut each celery blade into 1-inch (2.5-cm) chunks.
- Wipe the mushrooms with a clean cloth and cut them in half.
- Peel and cut the onion in half,

then each half into 4 or 5 pieces; separate the pieces.
- Open the tins of tomatoes and the wine.
- Mix the mace and salt in a cup and put to hand for seasoning the chicken pieces.
- Heat all the oil in a large heavy-bottomed non-stick frying pan, until well smoking. Using tongs, or a palette knife and cook's fork, put in the leg pieces 6 or so at a time and fry these to a good golden-brown on each side, sprinkling them with a little of the salt and mace before turning

them. Allow 2–3 minutes on each side. Remove the pieces to a kitchen tray or dish, whilst you brown the remaining pieces, maintaining the high heat and remembering to season each piece. Discard any remaining fats.

- Using a straight-edged wooden spatula to stir things, melt the oil and butter in a large flameproof casserole, stirring it around as you do so to ensure the even mixing and heating of the two.
- Add the onion, celery. Crush the garlic and add it, and let these lightly brown over a high heat, stirring them frequently. This will take 4–5 minutes. Add the mushrooms and fry these for a further minute or so.
- Sprinkle over the flour and mix very well in whilst you continue to fry.
- Turn off the heat.
- Sprinkle over and mix in the salt, pepper and sugar. Add the piece of lemon rind and the thyme. Add the tomatoes and wine.
- Turn on the heat, bring this 'sauce' to boiling point and allow it to bubble fairly rapidly for a minute or so, stirring and making sure that the mixture isn't sticking to the bottom of the pan by pushing the spatula right across the bottom. If you are preparing

this the day before, then allow to cool and refrigerate.
- Snip the parsley (see p.132), cover with plastic film and refrigerate.

▤ *P*re-dinner cooking
(1¾ hours)

- Pre-heat the oven to Gas Mark 4, Electricity 350°F or 180°C.
- Over a *low* heat, bring the sauce to boiling point in the casserole, add the leg joints, then arrange the breast pieces on top. Cover with a lid and transfer the dish to the oven.
- Cook for 1¼–1½ hours taking the breast pieces out on to a plate after 30 minutes, returning them for 5 minutes to heat through at the end.
- Cut the spring onions into 1-inch (2.5-cm) lengths and add these at the end at the same time as the chicken, and stir them well in.

▤ *F*inishing touches

- Just before serving, wipe the edge of the dish clean and sprinkle over the parsley.

▤ *A*ccompaniments

- Serve with plain boiled rice or creamed potatoes.
- White Burgundy or a light claret go well with this.

Pan-Fried
Breasts of Duckling with a
Mustard and Rum Cream Sauce

'*M*agrets' or duck breasts can now be bought in most top supermarkets. Here's an exotic way of preparing them. You can prepare the marinade and marinate them the morning before.

Ingredients

6 boneless duck breasts (magrets)

1 teaspoon salt
1 teaspoon black pepper

Marinade

1 clove garlic, crushed
4 Tablespoons good olive oil
2 Tablespoons soy sauce
2 heaped teaspoons mild Dijon mustard
2 teaspoons ground coriander

Sauce

4 fl ozs (100 ml) Demerara rum *or* brandy
1 heaped teaspoon mild French mustard
¼ pint (150 ml) tinned chicken consommé
⅓ pint (190 ml) single cream
salt, pepper

*A*dvance preparation
(15 minutes + 2 hours for marinating)

- Trim the breasts of excess fat. Using a sharp knife, make diagonal incisions across the skin ¼-inch (.5-cm) deep into the flesh, and at ½-inch (1-cm) intervals. Turn the breasts over, and make similar shallow incisions into the flesh. Lay the breasts, skin-side down, on a meat dish or other suitable platter.
- Mix all the ingredients for the marinade in a bowl. Spoon over each breast. Cover the dish with plastic film and leave to marinate, refrigerated, for 1 hour or more. Turn the breasts over and leave them for 1 further hour.

*P*re-dinner cooking
(30–40 minutes)

- Pre-heat a non-stick frying pan and seal the duck breasts over a high heat on both sides. Do 3 at a time. Lower the heat to medium and continue frying the duck breasts for 10–12 minutes for pink, 20–25 minutes for well done, turning the breasts at 2-minute intervals. As they are cooked, transfer them to a warm serving dish and keep them hot in the oven at Gas Mark ¼, Electricity 225°F or 110°C.

- Fry the second batch of 3 in the same way.
- Have ready at the side of the stove, the rum, mustard, consommé, cream, salt and pepper.
- Pour away all but ½ Tablespoon of excess fat in the frying pan. Set the pan back over a low heat. Using a wooden spatula, smear in the heaped teaspoon of mustard; when it gets hot and is taking on a brown colour, pour in the rum. There will be much sizzling and steaming. Watch this subside.
- Pour in the stock. Let the modest amount of liquid start to reduce.

Work the sediments into the sauce whilst it bubbles fairly rapidly. Pour in the cream. Bubble until viscous.

- Strain into a clean pan through a fine-meshed strainer.
- Bring the sauce back to the boil and spoon around the waiting duck breasts. If there are any pink juices on the plate, pour these into the sauce and whisk in. If you make the sauce before your guests sit at table, don't re-heat, and spoon it over the portions until you are ready to serve it.

≡ *Accompaniments*
- Serve with boiled noodles.
- Try a very fruity Zinfandel with this.

Chicken Vinaigrette

I used to make this with mayonnaise—and still do, as folk love it—but for the diet-conscious a vinaigrette is better. It makes an ideal summer main course, and can be prepared the evening before and refrigerated.

≡ Ingredients

1 boiled chicken (see p.137)
4 blades celery, washed, chopped
1 small can peaches, drained
6 plump spring onions, trimmed
1 small can water chestnuts, drained

½ pint (275 ml) Rich French Dressing (see p. 138)

≡ Garnish
2 Tablespoons chopped parsley *or* mint (see p.132)
4 tomatoes

▒*A*dvance preparation
(1½–1¾ hours)

- Boil the chicken (see p.137) and allow to cool.
- While the chicken is cooling, trim the spring onions leaving as much green on as you can, and slice these thinly on the diagonal.
- Slice the peaches and cut to size.
- Slice the water chestnuts.
- Skin and chop the tomatoes (see p.135) and put to one side.
- Snip the parsley (see p.132) and put to one side.
- Cut the celery into diagonal strips about ¼-inch (.5-cm) thick.
- Refrigerate each item in a separate plastic bag to avoid 'cross-flavouring'.
- Prepare the French Dressing (see p.138) and keep in the fridge until required.
- The most important part of this recipe is to make sure all the bits of gristle and skin are removed from the chicken, and that the chicken is cut into attractive, small, bite-size pieces. Pull off all the skin and discard. Break off the legs at the thigh where it joins the carcass. Pull off the skin. Using a small knife, cut down the breast bone and take off the breasts. Pull off any meat still adhering to the carcass. Pull the drumstick from the thigh at the natural joint. Pull and cut off the meat from the thighs and drumsticks, using a small knife.
- Using a cook's knife, cut the breasts into ¼-inch (.5-cm) thick strips on the diagonal. Put these into a large mixing bowl. Cut the leg meat lengthwise, i.e. with the grain, into same-size pieces.
- Refrigerate the chicken pieces, covered with plastic film.

▒*P*re-dinner preparation
(5–10 minutes)

- Mix the chicken, onions, peaches, chestnuts and celery in a salad bowl.
- Pour the French Dressing over adding more if you like things very moist.
- Scatter over the chopped tomatoes and sprinkle over the parsley or mint.

▒*A*ccompaniment

- Try a Rosé from Provence with this.

104

Vegetables

Contents

Vegetables

I wonder if the tendency for us to overcook our vegetables is still with us? I don't think so. Today, with the emphasis on healthier eating, we are beginning to enjoy vegetables cooked crisp, allowing the individual flavour of each to speak for itself. But to follow this practice does mean split-second timing in the kitchen, and that you stand by at the stove ready to drain them the second they are 'al dente'—crisp to the tooth, that is.

The recipes I have chosen for you can be prepared and kept warm; at least for the 20 minutes or so you will spend eating your first course.

I too can become somewhat harassed when I have guests for dinner; on busy weekdays I may not be back at the house until seven in the evening. This problem is easily solved. I serve tiny jacket potatoes with cream or butter—or Greek yoghurt for the faint-hearted—and a tossed salad of those mixed green leaves which are becoming available in all good food stores.

Glazed Carrots in
Apple Juice and Ginger

*T*his is an easy and very effective recipe. Cooking in apple juice rather than water may come as a surprise. Good, it's meant to! This dish can be kept warm without harming for up to ½ hour.

Ingredients

2 lbs (900 grams) same-size carrots
¾ pint (425 ml) or more apple juice
2 ozs (50 grams) butter

2 teaspoons caster sugar
1 heaped teaspoon ground ginger
1 level teaspoon salt
2–3 teaspoons lemon juice

*A*dvance preparation
(20–25 minutes)

- Top, tail and peel the carrots. Slice them in a food processor, or on a mandoline, or laboriously by hand, into the thinnest discs possible.
- Pack them into a saucepan.
- Just cover with the apple juice and add the butter and caster sugar.
- Leave them like this until you are ready to cook them. They can be cut, morning for evening.

*P*re-dinner cooking
(30 minutes)

- Put the vegetable tureen to warm in the oven (turned on very low).
- Bring the carrots to the boil, without a lid. Lower the heat to medium and cook the carrots for 5 minutes for crisp, a further 4–5 minutes for tender.
- Drain them through a fine-meshed sieve set over a pan or bowl.
- Return the carrots to the saucepan. Cover them with a lid and set aside.
- Add the ginger to the liquid and reduce this to about half a teacupful of buttery, syrupy glaze by boiling rapidly. This can take up to 20 minutes, depending on the size of your pan which will dictate the speed at which the liquid evaporates. Be patient, it *will* reduce.
- The pan will look very tarnished round the sides. Take the pan from the heat. Taste the syrup—it will be sweetish—adding a very little salt and the odd teaspoon or two of lemon juice to spike it up a little.

*F*inishing touches

- Mix the syrup with the carrots and turn them into the warm tureen.

Quick Braised
Endive Spears with
Gruyère or Parmesan Cheese

*T*his recipe calls for stock. No busy person has a stock pot today. Canned consommé makes a more than good substitute, and no one will know, unless you tell them. Much of this dish can be prepared the night before.

Ingredients

12 small, same size, spears of Belgian endive
2 teaspoons caster sugar

1 tin Batchelor's double-strength consommé
2 ozs (50 grams) grated Gruyère *or* Parmesan cheese

Advance preparation
(25 minutes)

- Trim the brown bits off the endive root ends. Pull off any tarnished leaves.
- Bring to the boil a large saucepan of water to which you have added the sugar. Tip in the endive and boil this rapidly for 5 minutes. This will blanch them.
- Tip them into a colander. Cool them under cold running water for 3–4 minutes. Allow them to drain. Pat away excess moisture with kitchen towels.
- Butter a shallow ovenproof dish and arrange the blanched endive in this, thick ends outwards, points to the centre, in roughly one layer: they can jostle and overlap a bit.
- Spoon over the consommé, and dredge evenly with whatever cheese you are using.
- If you are not going to cook them immediately, you will find that the endive discolour slightly, looking greyish, but this is of little consequence. Cover the dish with plastic film and store in the fridge.

Last-minute cooking
(20 minutes)

- Pre-heated the oven to Gas Mark 6, Electricity 400°F or 200°C. Bake, uncovered, for 10–15 minutes, when they will be nicely browned and bubbling.
- If you need to keep them hot for more than 10 minutes or so, cover with a lid or a piece of foil; if you do so, the cheese will go soft but will be O.K.

Finishing touches
- Serve in the dish.

Tiny New Potatoes
with Cream and Nutmeg

Selecting even-sized potatoes means that they will all be cooked at the same time. The cream and nutmeg make them exotic and are simple to add. As a variation, you can add unsalted butter, chives and parsley. (The use of chives plus a second green herb is very effective—the light oniony aromatic acting as a perfect foil for the more scented herb.)

Potatoes can be cooked at least ½ hour ahead of time, if wished, although I have prescribed 'Last-Minute Cooking' here.

Ingredients

2 lbs (900 grams) graded baby new
    potatoes
2 teaspoons salt
¼ pint (150 ml) double cream
1 level teaspoon ground nutmeg

Variation (instead of cream and nutmeg)

3 ozs (75 grams) unsalted butter
2 Tablespoons chopped chives and chopped
    mint *or* chopped parsley

Advance preparation
(5–10 minutes)

- Scrub the potatoes well, leaving their skins on.
- Rinse them in a sieve under the cold tap.
- Put them in a saucepan large enough to leave 3–4 inches' (8–10 cms') space above water level, so that they won't boil over.
- Cover the potatoes with cold water, add the salt and set them aside until ready to cook.

Last-minute cooking
(12 minutes)

- Put the vegetable serving dish to warm.
- Set the saucepan over a good heat and bring it to the boil.
- Adjust the heat so that the potatoes are boiling gently. (I suggest that you leave the lid off if only as a reminder that they need your attention.)
- After 10–12 minutes, test a potato to see whether it is cooked. It should be.

- Stand a colander in the sink and tip the potatoes in. If there is any scum on them, rinse off under the hot tap.
- Set the saucepan back over a low heat, pour in the cream, sprinkle over the nutmeg and mix in by swirling the pan around. Allow to bubble for a few seconds.
- Add the drained potatoes, put on the lid and swirl and toss them in the hot cream until each potato is well coated.
- As a variation, omit the cream and substitute the unsalted butter. Take care when melting and warming the butter that it does not brown; do it over a low heat.
- Sprinkle on the chopped herbs.

*F*inishing touches
- Transfer to a heated, lidded vegetable dish.

French Beans in a Hot Vinaigrette

*T*his way of serving French beans makes a delightful change.

Ingredients

2 × 8-oz (225-gram) packets of frozen whole French beans
1 teaspoon salt

¼ pint (150 ml) French Dressing (see p.138)
2 heaped Tablespoons snipped chives *or* parsley (p.132)

*A*dvance preparation
(6 minutes)
- Overnight defrost the beans on the bottom shelf of the fridge and drain. I know the packages say to cook beans from frozen. I don't.
- Prepare the French Dressing (see p.138).

*P*re-dinner cooking
(15 minutes)
- Snip the chives or parsley.
- Two-thirds fill a large lidded pan with water and bring it rapidly to the boil: add a generous teaspoon of salt.
- Tip the beans in and cook for only 2–3 minutes.
- Stand a colander in the sink. Tip the beans into this.
- Return the pan to the hob, pour in the French Dressing.
- Add the well-drained beans. Put on the lid and toss them over the heat until very hot, holding the lid on firmly and tossing vigorously.
- Sprinkle in the herbs, and toss.

Baby Jacket
Potatoes with Herb Butter

Ingredients

18–24 small, even-sized potatoes

Herb Butter (see p.140)

Advance preparation
(5–10 minutes)

- Prepare your Herb Butter (p.140) and keep it in the fridge.

Pre-dinner cooking
(30 minutes)

- Pre-heat the oven to Gas Mark 9—yes, 9—or Electricity 475°F or 240°C.
- Have ready a basket lined with a napkin.
- Have discs of herb butter in an attractive bowl of iced water ready in the refrigerator.
- The secret here is to select small even-sized potatoes. These should be no more than 2 inches (5 cms) in diameter.
- Allow 3–4 potatoes per serving. Scrub them. Brush them all over with soy oil.
- Line a baking tray with foil (they may well drop between the bars of your oven rack). Arrange the potatoes an inch apart on this. Bake the potatoes for about 20 minutes, when they will be really crisp and fluffy.
- Lower the heat to Gas Mark ½ (Electricity 250°F or 130°C) and leave them where they are until you are ready to serve them.

Baby
Minted Peas

*F*rozen peas can be a delight or a disaster. I have found that the frozen petit pois behave very well if you follow my method here which requires no water.

Ingredients

12-oz (350-gram) bag frozen petits pois
2 ozs (50 grams) unsalted butter
1 level teaspoon salt

2 level teaspoons caster sugar
1 Tablespoon finely snipped garden mint leaves

≣ *A*dvance preparation
- Allow the peas to defrost in the bottom of the refrigerator overnight.

≣ *L*ast-minute cooking
                    (3–4 minutes)
- Warm the serving dish at the oven's lowest temperature.
- Snip the mint in the same way as parsley (p.132).
- Melt the butter in a medium-sized lidded, heavy-bottomed saucepan.
- Add the defrosted peas, salt and sugar. Put the lid on. *You do not need any water.*
- Over a low heat, toss the peas until hot through and the liquid is bubbling. This takes only a few minutes. The peas will be bright green, buttery and just tender.
- Stir in the snipped mint.

≣ *F*inishing touches
- Transfer to the warm serving dish. The peas can be served in their buttery juice, or transferred to the serving dish with a slotted spoon.

Simple
Tomato Salad

*T*his can be prepared the morning before.

≣ Ingredients

6 large even-sized tomatoes *or* 3
   beefsteak tomatoes

¼ pint (150 ml) French Dressing
2 Tablespoons chopped parsley or chives
   (see p.132) *or* fresh torn basil leaves

≣ *A*dvance preparation
                    (15–20 minutes)
- Skin the tomatoes (see p.135).
- Make up the French Dressing (see p.138).
- Chop the parsley (p.132) or snip the chives (see p.131).
- Cut the tomatoes into ¼-inch (.5-cm) thick slices. Gently fan each open somewhat with the palm of the hand.
- Lift each group of slices on to small plates or one larger dish (in the case of the beefsteak tomatoes apportion these logically).
- The tomatoes can be sliced, plated, covered with plastic film, and refrigerated.

≣ *F*inishing touch
- Mix the chosen herb with the dressing and spoon over the tomatoes just before serving.

Mashed and Creamed Potatoes

*D*on't ever underestimate people's love of good creamed potatoes. They go with anything, almost, and are gaining rapidly in the popularity stakes, particularly if you make them as I do. Once cooked, they can be kept happily for about 1 hour.

Ingredients

3 lbs (1.3 kg) *or* about 6 large, even-sized potatoes
2 teaspoons salt
4 ozs (100 grams) good quality, unsalted butter cut into cubes

1 level teaspoon nutmeg
1 level teaspoon milled pepper

Variation (instead of butter)

¼ pint (150 grams) double cream

*A*dvance preparation
(15 minutes)

- Peel the potatoes, cut them in half lengthways, and in half again, also lengthways. Put them in a saucepan, cover them with cold water an inch above the tops. Add the salt.

*L*ast-minute cooking
(30 minutes)

- Put a lidded vegetable tureen to warm.
- Bring the saucepan to the boil over a high heat. When boiling, lower the heat to medium so that they are gently boiling. No lid is needed. Allow 20 minutes from cold.
- Test them for doneness using a skewer or the point of a knife. A 4-pronged fork will break them.

- Drain into a colander, set in the sink. Return the potatoes to the pan, and, over a low heat dry them out for 1–2 minutes, tossing them over the heat with the lid on.
- Add the butter, nutmeg and milled pepper.
- Mash them well with a potato masher (a food processor will turn them into a glutinous mess.)
- Use a balloon whisk, or 4-pronged dinner fork as a final touch for whipping them to a light texture.
- If you are using cream instead of butter, heat the cream in a separate non-stick saucepan. Beat it into the potatoes after you have mashed them.
- Pile the potato into the warm lidded tureen and keep warm in the oven at Gas Mark ¼, Electricity 225°F or 110°C.

Leaf Spinach with
Soured Cream and Garlic

*T*his makes a tasty addition to any main course—and is quick to prepare.

Ingredients

2 lbs (900 grams) spinach
2 ozs (50 grams) butter *or* soy oil
1 clove garlic, crushed

1 teaspoon salt
1 level teaspoon milled pepper
½ level teaspoon ground nutmeg
¼-pint (150-ml) carton soured cream

*A*dvance preparation
(15 minutes)

- Cut off the stalks of the spinach and discard.
- Fill the sink with cold water and wash the spinach well, letting the grit sink to the bottom.
- Lift it out and drain well on the draining board.
- Refrigerate until ready.

*P*re-dinner cooking
(5–10 minutes)

- In a large lidded pan, melt the butter but do not let it brown, so swirl the pan around over a lowish heat.

- Crush the garlic in the garlic press into the pan and warm it for a minute or two: taking the pan away from the heat if it starts to fry.
- Pack on the spinach. Season with salt, pepper and nutmeg.
- Put on the lid and 'wilt' the spinach over a medium heat. It will 'sink' when it does. Stir things around until it is just tender (about 3–4 minutes).
- Pour away the juices (or retain for a soup or gravy).
- Dribble the soured cream over. Put the lid back on and *just* heat things through.

113

Stir-Fried Brussels Sprouts or '50-Second Sprouts'

*T*hese really are cooked in 50 seconds. Well, 60 perhaps! and will convert any sprout-loather, as they taste so crisp and fresh.

Ingredients

1 lb (450 grams) small sprouts
2 Tablespoons olive oil *or* soy oil
1 clove garlic

1 level teaspoon ground nutmeg
1 level teaspoon ground black pepper
1 teaspoon caster sugar
½ teaspoon salt

Advance preparation
(10 minutes)

- Trim and wash the sprouts.
- Fit the metal slicing blade (not the shredder) to a food processor and finely slice the sprouts. Turn them into a bowl. (Covered with plastic film, you can store it in the fridge for a short time.)
- Skin the garlic and crush it in the garlic press.
- Warm the vegetable tureen.

Last-minute cooking
(50–60 seconds)

- Have everything at the ready.
- In a wok or in a large deep pan, heat the oil until lightly smoking.
- Stir in the garlic and fry for 3–4 seconds only.
- Using a large fork, gradually add the shredded sprouts. Stir and mix well over a brisk heat, working deftly and seasoning with the nutmeg, pepper, sugar and salt as you go along. Stir and fry for 50 seconds or until the sprouts *just* wilt, but are very hot.

Finishing touches

- Turn into the heated tureen and serve.

Puddings

Contents

*I*n spite of healthier eating, I still contend that a little bit of what you fancy is a better pick-u-up than any psychiatrist's couch! That excuse over with, I introduce the puddings.

To present a hot pudding can bring that 'gosh factor' to your party, and if that hot pudding is a new version of an old favourite, then you're going to be cook-of-the-week in the eyes of those friends who claim of their partner 'she (or he!) never makes a good pudding these days'.

Cream—and cool, rich, thick, double cream to boot—is always the perfect foil to any pudding, but it *is* optional; strained Greek yoghurt can be an acceptable alternative. Or, time permitting, a tangy fresh raspberry sauce is foolproof, easy to make in advance and is an excellent accompaniment to all the hot puddings I give.

A dish of chilled cooked fruit is never amiss as long as that all-essential element of surprise is present: rose-flower water with the deceptively simple poached apples, or vanilla with the fresh peaches. Also in the section on cold sweets, I have given a face-lift to that golden oldie, rice pudding, going back unashamedly to those 18th-century cookbooks again where cream, egg yolks and fruits were in the list of ingredients to make a sublime confection for you to enjoy.

Chocolate Chip Sponge Pudding with a Raspberry Sauce and Soured Cream

*T*his dark toned but light and fluffy sponge pudding is not to be restricted to the colder months any more than a hot soufflé. In fact, it is lighter textured than many a soufflé I've had! I make this pudding in the summer, and instead of chocolate chips I scatter in a small punnet of fresh raspberries, which creates great excitement among my guests!

Ingredients

4 ozs (100 grams) unsalted butter
4 ozs (100 grams) caster sugar
2 teaspoons vanilla essence
2 large eggs
4 ozs (100 grams) plain white flour
2 ozs (50 grams) cocoa powder
2 heaped teaspoons baking powder
2 ozs (50 grams) bitter chocolate

Raspberry Sauce

8 ozs (225 grams) frozen raspberries
2 ozs (50 grams)—or slightly less—caster sugar
juice 1 lemon

Serving

⅓ pint (190 ml) soured cream

Pre-dinner cooking
(2 hours)

- Butter generously a 1½-pint (1-litre) pudding basin or mould.
- Cream the butter and sugar in a bowl until light and fluffy.
- Add the vanilla essence.
- Sift together the flour, cocoa and baking powder twice, on to a paper.

- Beat the eggs in a separate bowl then beat them into the pudding mixture. If they show signs of splitting and curdling, add a small spoonful of the flour.
- Thoroughly cut and fold in the remaining flour and cocoa mixture using a little cold water to arrive at a loose-dropping consistency. (This means that the

mixture drops away from the spoon or spatula as soon as it is held up from the bowl.)
- Break and crush the chocolate into ¼ inch (.5 cm) chips and stir them well into the mixture.
- Spoon the mixture into the buttered basin and cover with buttered foil. Make a pleat in the foil and tie down with string.
- Select a saucepan large enough to hold the basin and half-fill with water. Bring the water to the boil and place the basin inside.
- Steam the pudding with the water boiling at a steady roll for 1½–2 hours. Add more boiling water if necessary.
- As soon as the pudding is on the boil, you can make the Raspberry Sauce. Toss all the ingredients together in a saucepan over a low heat until the juices from the raspberries draw. Press and rub through a fine sieve. Chill well or serve hot.

▤ *F*inishing touches
- Run a palette knife round the sides of the basin, invert it and turn the pudding out on to a serving dish. Remove the paper. Serve immediately, accompanied by a bowl of soured cream and with the chilled Raspberry Sauce. Or you can heat the sauce over a low heat in a saucepan and serve it hot.

▤ *A*ccompaniments
- Try some Madeira with this.

Coffee, Walnut and Date Pudding with Apricot Sauce

*T*his slots into the stickier end of puddings and will be received with smiles of delight.

▤ Ingredients

Pudding

4 ozs (100 grams) unsalted butter
4 ozs (100 grams) caster sugar
2 eggs
1 level teaspoon instant coffee dissolved in
    1 Tablespoon boiling water and cooled
4 ozs (100 grams) self-raising flour

2 ozs (50 grams) walnuts
4 ozs (100 grams) dates
2 Tablespoons rum

▤ Apricot Sauce

2 ozs (50 grams) caster sugar
1 teaspoon vanilla essence
8 ozs (225 grams) apricot jam

Advance preparation
(overnight soaking + 15 minutes)
- Roughly chop the dates and overnight soak them in the rum.
- Beat the eggs.
- Dissolve the instant coffee in 1 Tablespoon of boiling water and allow to cool.
- Sieve the flour.
- Chop the walnuts roughly.

Pre-dinner cooking
(2 hours)
- Generously butter a 2-pint (or 1-litre) pudding basin or mould. Put a small circle of buttered paper in the bottom.
- Cream the butter and sugar until light and fluffy.
- Beat the eggs and add them a little at a time. Add the coffee essence.
- Fold in the sieved flour, then the nuts and dates and the modest amount of rum.
- Spoon the mixture into the basin. Level the top. Cover with buttered foil, making a 1-inch (2.5-cm) pleat and tying down well.
- Steam for 2 hours, as described in the previous recipe, over gently boiling water. Top up the pan at frequent intervals with more water.
- While it is steaming make the Apricot Sauce: Bring the sugar, vanilla essence and 4 fl ozs (100 ml) water to the boil and simmer until clear and syrupy.
- In a second smaller pan: Put in the jam and half the syrup. Then, stirring all the time, bring to the boil over a low heat. Press through a hair sieve; adjust the consistency using more of the syrup. Serve hot or cold.
- If the sauce is to be served cold it will require more syrup, added when the purée is quite cold. Lemon juice, rum, kirsch or any other liqueur can be added for extra flavouring.

Finishing touches
- When the pudding is cooked, run a palette knife round the sides of the basin and invert on to a warm serving dish. Remove the disc of paper. Serve with the Apricot Sauce, thick cream or custard.

Accompaniment
- Serve Barsac with this.

Rich Bread and Butter Pudding

*M*y first efforts to update this national pudding appeared in the *Yorkshire Post* almost 15 years ago, when I used a milk custard, but still included quite a lot of bread *cubes* and certainly too much

118

jam. More recently, in *Just Desserts* for BBC Pebble Mill, I lightened it still further. Here, I have gone as far as I think it possible without losing sight of its name. Bread is at a minimum, the light rich custard is made with cream, the fruit is liquor-soaked and the modest amount of jam is sieved. The result? . . . . *ambrosia*!

Ingredients

6 ozs (175 grams) sultanas
2 Tablespoons brandy *or* whisky
2½ ozs (approx. 60 grams) softened, unsalted butter
8 slices white bread
4 ozs (100 grams) apricot jam

½ pint (275 ml) double cream
½ pint (275 ml) milk
5 large eggs
2 ozs (50 grams) caster sugar
1 teaspoon vanilla essence
¼–½ teaspoon grated nutmeg
icing sugar for dredging

Advance preparation
(15–20 minutes + overnight soaking)

- Put the sultanas into a small bowl, pour over the brandy or whisky and leave to soak, covered, for 4 hours or overnight. (This is not imperative: rather a nice luxury.)
- Take a 9–10-inch (23–25-cm) diameter dish or oblong ovenproof dish, 1½–2-inches (4–7.5-cm) deep. Well butter the sides and bottom using a good knob of the softened butter and a pad of kitchen paper towel.
- Cut the crusts off the bread and discard.
- Spread each piece with some of the remaining 2 ozs (50 grams) butter, using it all up.
- Press the apricot jam through a sieve and make the bread and

butter into sandwiches using the jam. Cut each sandwich in half, and each half into 3 pieces.
- Scatter the sultanas in.
- Arrange the sandwiches on the base of the dish each slightly overlapping the other in rows if using a rectangular dish, in concentric circles if using a round one.
- Refrigerate if you are not proceeding with the cooking immediately.

Pre-dinner cooking
(1–1¼ hours)

- Preheat the oven to Gas Mark 3, Electricity 325°F or 170°C. Arrange the shelf a rung or two above the centre of the oven.
- Select a second ovenproof dish or roasting tin of a size to contain the

one holding the pudding mixture. Do a test and pour in enough water to come a little more than halfway up the sides of the baking dish. Then remove this, wiping it dry with paper towels.

- Put the dish or tin containing the water into the oven.
- Break 3 of the eggs into a 2-pint (or 1-litre) Pyrex basin. Separate the yolks of the 2 remaining eggs (see p.129) and add these to the basin. Place the basin on a folded damp J-cloth to stop it skidding, and, using a balloon whisk, mix the eggs, sugar and vanilla. Whisk rapidly until quite creamy (for about 2 minutes).
- Rinse out a non-stick pan with cold water. Pour in the milk and cream and bring to the boil over a medium heat. Stir it a couple of times with the whisk to ensure even heating, and watch that it doesn't suddenly boil over. When the milk mixture starts to hiss and rise up the sides of the pan, pour it slowly over the egg mixture whilst whisking and stirring with the balloon whisk in the other hand. Mix thoroughly for a few seconds. You have just made a light custard. Well done!
- Now, using a ladle, cover the bread pieces with the custard allowing it to soak into each piece as you pour over each ladleful.
- Have some nutmeg in a teaspoon and using finger and thumb sprinkle about ¼ teaspoon over the surface of the pudding (use more if you like nutmeg a lot).
- Open the oven door. Using oven gloves or two kitchen towels

folded comfortably, pick up the pudding dish and set it in the tin containing the water (known as a bain-marie). Bake for 45 minutes to 1 hour (the exact time will depend on the size and type of your oven) or until the 'custard' is *just* set and the bread is lightly browned.

- Remove the pudding from the bain-marie.
- Lay a few pieces of kitchen paper on a work surface. Remove the pudding and stand the dish on this to absorb the water.
- Stand a small fine-meshed sieve on a piece of paper. Put 2 heaped teaspoons of icing sugar into this. Dredge the surface of the pudding liberally with this. Wipe the edges of the dish and stand it on a platter for ease of carrying.
- Whilst best served as soon as it is baked, little harm will come to it if it has to wait for 30 minutes or so in the oven with the heat off.
- If you use the same dish, recipe, temperature and method, noting the exact time it took to set, you can gauge things accurately by using a pinger or timer each time. What you cannot gauge is how long you are going to chat over the main course! Don't be tempted to use a higher temperature or abandon the bain-marie, or the custard may curdle.

Accompaniments
- Serve with hot or warm thick pouring cream or strained Greek yoghurt *and* an Apricot Sauce on special occasions (p.117).
- Drink a glass of Sauternes with this.

Apple, Almond and Cinnamon Crumble

*T*his can be prepared 2 to 3 days ahead and kept in the fridge to be finished off at the last minute.

Ingredients

2½–3 lbs (1–1.4 kg) Cox's apples
3–4 strips orange zest
strained juice of 1 orange
2 ozs (50 grams) unsalted butter
1½–2 ozs (30–50 grams) caster sugar
1 level teaspoon ground cinnamon

Topping

3 ozs (75 grams) cold unsalted butter
4 ozs (100 grams) self-raising flour
2 ozs (50 grams) caster sugar
2 ozs (50 grams) ground almonds
2 × 5-gram packets flaked *or* nibbed almonds

*A*dvance preparation
(30–40 minutes)

- Peel, core, quarter and slice the apples.
- Take the zest off the orange with a potato peeler, taking care not to dig into the pith. Put to one side. Halve the orange and squeeze the juice into a large saucepan.
- Add the first 2 ozs (50 grams) of butter.
- Put the apple slices into the pan.
- Scatter over sugar and cinnamon, add the pieces of orange zest, and mix in. Put on the lid.
- Stand the pan over a low heat and gradually bring things to the boil, holding the lid on and tossing the contents hard 2 or 3 times. Cook the apples to a soft pulp: this will take about 15 minutes.
- Take off the lid. Leave the mixture to cool completely. Take out the pieces of orange zest and discard. Mash roughly with a fork. Put into a bowl, cover and refrigerate till needed.
- To make the topping, dice the second quantity of butter into very small cubes (about ¼ inch/.5 cm), and rub them into the flour between the fingertips, lifting the hands up and above the basin as you rub, letting it fall back as you do so. Continue doing this until you have a moist, sand-like texture. Using a fork, mix in the sugar, ground almonds and flaked almonds. Put into a plastic bag in the fridge until required.

*L*ast-minute cooking
(20–25 minutes)

- Pre-heat the oven to Gas Mark 6, Electricity 400°F or 200°C.
- Spoon the apple mixture into a 9 × 3 × 4 inches-deep (23 × 7·5 × 10 cm) ovenproof dish. Sprinkle over the topping.
- Bake on a shelf in the middle of

the oven for 20–25 minutes or until the topping is crisp and golden-brown. If it shows signs of really burning as opposed to browning, turn down the heat a notch.

≋ Accompaniments
- Accompany this with thick cream or yoghurt.
- Serve a Gewurztraminer wine.

Cold Puddings

Poached Peaches in a Vanilla and Orange Syrup

*T*his deceptively simple recipe will impress your guests with its subtle clean undertones. It can be prepared well beforehand.

≋ Ingredients
6 large ripe peaches

≋ Syrup
½ pint (275 ml) water

4 Tablespoons caster sugar
1 teaspoon grated orange zest
2 teaspoons vanilla extract *or* essence *or* 2-inch (5-cm) piece of vanilla pod

≋ *A*dvance preparation
(20 minutes)
- Have ready a large pan of gently boiling water and a large bowl of cold water. Using a slotted spoon, plunge two peaches at a time into the boiling water, count to 10 slowly, then remove them to the cold water. Do this with all the peaches. Take a small pointed knife and cut round the peach following the natural line on the fruit. Gently twist the two halves apart. Take out the stone. Scrape or peel off the skin. If the peaches are very ripe, and this can be a slippery job, use a piece of kitchen paper to help hold them.
- In a small pan make the syrup by bringing the water, sugar, zest and vanilla extract to the boil. Simmer for 1 minute or so until all the sugar is dissolved.
- In a large shallow enamel or stainless steel sauté pan (a meticulously clean frying pan will do), arrange the peach halves in one layer. Pour over the syrup, bring to the boil, lower the heat and simmer the fruit for 5 minutes, or until tender.
- Remove the peaches with a draining spoon to a glass serving bowl. Return the pan with the

syrup to the heat and bubble this down until you only have ¼ pint (150 ml) of syrupy liquid left. Allow this to cool for 10 minutes or so before straining over the peaches through a small wire mesh strainer. Cool. Cover with plastic film and chill.

Accompaniments
- Serve plain, or with fromage frais, ice cream, strained Greek yoghurt or delicious thick yellow double cream!
- Try with this a light Sauternes or Barsac or, if the pocket permits, one of the golden-toned Auslesens from Germany.

Alternatives
- You can substitute pears for peaches. Knife-peel, halve and core the pears and cook till tender in the syrup.

Compôte of Kumquats with Whisky

Kumquats are those tiny oval-shaped fruit that look like mini-oranges. Their flavour is deliciously exotic, and they're simple to prepare. The kumquats will keep for weeks refrigerated so can be prepared well in advance.

Ingredients

1½ lbs (675 grams) kumquats
8 ozs (225 grams) caster sugar

½ pint (275 ml) cold water
4 Tablespoons whisky

Advance preparation
(35 minutes)
- Wash the kumquats in a sieve under running cold water. Pick off any bits of stalk which may be on them.
- In a large (4-pint or 2-litre) pan, bring the sugar and water to the boil, lower the heat and simmer until the liquid is clear. Tip in the whole fruits, cover with a lid and simmer for about 30 minutes or until tender, stirring them with a wooden spoon from time to time. Add the whisky when they're cooked.
- Leave them to cool in the pan.
- Spoon them into a serving dish, cover with plastic film. Chill well.

Accompaniments
- Serve with strained Greek yoghurt, ice cream, or fresh double cream.
- A glass of chilled Cointreau will go beautifully with this.

Rich Rice Pudding (Chilled or Hot)

*A*ll the ingredients of a traditional 18th-century rice pudding are here brought back together again and enriched with cream. I like it best served cold, studded with candied or crystallized fruits. The subtle complement of an extra spoonful of *unsweetened* thick chilled cream is worth breaking the diet rules for.

Ingredients

1 pint (570 ml) milk
3 ozs (75 grams) Carolina (pudding) rice, washed
2 ozs (50 grams) caster sugar (or less)
1/4 teaspoon grated nutmeg
1 teaspoon grated lemon zest
1 teaspoon pure vanilla essence (or pod)
2 ozs (50 grams) candied orange
2 Tablespoons whisky

1 pint (570 ml) double *or* whipping cream
2 large egg yolks (see p.129) (if served hot)
1 level teaspoon gelatine crystals (if served cold)

Garnish

Other candied *or* fresh fruits, and/*or* flaked almonds (for cold)

*A*dvance preparation
   (1 hour 10 minutes + overnight soaking)

- Dice the candied fruit very small and soak overnight in the whisky.
- Put the milk, rice, sugar, nutmeg, lemon zest and vanilla into a lidded double-boiler. Boil until the rice is completely soft (about 45 minutes).
- If you are serving it hot, stir in the 2 egg yolks, candied fruit, and unwhipped cream. Transfer the pudding to a buttered 3–4-inch (8–10-cm) deep dish. Stand this in a baking tin half-filled with water and bake at Gas Mark 6, Electricity 400°F or 200°C for 20 minutes until the traditional skin is formed.
- If you are serving this cold, melt the gelatine in 2 Tablespoons of cold water and while the cooked rice is still hot stir the gelatine in thoroughly. Leave to cool.
- Gradually incorporate the candied fruit and the cream, which should be half-whipped to 'ribbon' stage, with a hand balloon whisk.

- Chill, covered with plastic film.

*F*inishing touches
- Serve hot with a Raspberry Sauce (see p. 116)
- Serve cold in a glass bowl garnished with extra candied fruits or flaked almonds. (The mixture will thicken somewhat as it chills.)

*A*ccompaniment
- Sauternes or Barsac go well with this.

Poached Apples in Rose-Flower Water and White Peppercorns

*T*his is not a mistake: the subtle spiciness of crushed white peppercorns is magical.

This can be prepared the evening or morning before.

Ingredients

6 medium, even-sized Cox's apples
juice 1 lemon, strained

Syrup

10 ozs (275 grams) caster sugar
2 teaspoons white peppercorns
1 level teaspoon ground coriander
2-inch (5-cm) plump piece fresh ginger

2 × 2-inch (5-cm) strips lemon zest
1 Tablespoon extra lemon juice
4 heaped dessertspoons sultanas
2 Tablespoons triple-strength rose-flower water (available from chemists)

Garnish (optional)

a few crystallized rose petals
2 ozs (50 grams) flaked almonds
1 tub strained Greek yoghurt

*A*dvance preparation
                (45 minutes)
- Remove the peel from the lemon with a swivel-blade potato peeler. Retain. Squeeze and strain the juice into a small basin.
- Peel the apples with a swivel-blade peeler, core them carefully with an apple corer, keeping them whole. Cut each apple into 5–6 ¼-inch (.5-cm) thick rings. Bathe or brush each ring with lemon juice to prevent tarnishing. Put the apples on to a dinner plate.
- Roughly crush the peppercorns. (You can do this with a rolling-pin on the work surface with the

peppercorns wrapped in the corner of a clean towel.)

- Peel and grate the ginger.
- In a 1½-pint (825-ml) stainless steel or enamel pan make the syrup by boiling together in ½-pint (275-ml) of water the sugar, peppercorns, coriander, ginger, 2 good pieces of the lemon zest and 1 Tablespoon of lemon juice. Bring to the boil and bubble well for 2–3 minutes.
- In a meticulously clean frying pan or wide, shallow sauté pan, arrange the apple rings in concentric circles, slightly overlapping and in one layer at a time (you will have to do 2 batches). Using a small conical sieve and a ladle, ladle over enough of the syrup to just cover the apple rings. Over a medium heat, bring things to the boil, lower the heat if necessary and gently poach the apples until just tender. This should only take about 2–3 minutes.
- Remove the first batch of poached apples one at a time to keep them whole, using a slotted spoon and arrange them in a shallow serving dish or platter. Poach the second layer in the remaining syrup, adding any you have left over. Remove these to the serving dish with the slotted spoon, letting them rest on top of the first layer.
- Add the rose-flower water to the still warm syrup in the pan, quickly stir in with a small balloon whisk.
- Add the sultanas, reheat to bubble, remove from the heat and leave the sultanas to plump up. Spoon the syrup over the apple rings to coat each one.
- Cool, covered with plastic film. Refrigerate to chill.

*F*inishing touches
- Scatter with a few crystallized rose petals and the flaked almonds. Don't do this more than 10 minutes before serving as commercial rose petals 'bleed' and stain. Pass the Greek yoghurt separately.

*A*ccompaniment
- Why not be brave and drink a glass of Gewurztraminer with this as a treat?

Apple Pie

If you've always heard that you should use cooking apples for an apple pie, try using a dessert apple such as a Cox instead. This can be cooked the day before, and can be served cold or re-heated.

Ingredients

2 lbs (900 ml) Cox's apples
1 lemon
2 ozs (50 grams) sugar, or to taste
2 ozs (50 grams) unsalted butter (for a hot pie)

Pastry

8 ozs (225 grams) plain white flour
3 ozs (75 grams) unsalted butter
2 ozs (50 grams) lard
2 heaped teaspoons icing sugar
2 Tablespoons cold water, mixed with
    1 Tablespoon lemon juice
1 egg

Advance preparation
(50–60 minutes)

- First the filling: peel, core, quarter, then slice the apples.
- Peel off 2 strips of zest from lemon and keep to one side. Cut the lemon in half and squeeze out all the juice and strain it.
- Toss the apple slices in the juice with the sugar and zest, in a lidded pan over a *low* heat (no water is used). Cook to a pulp.
- Remove the zest and discard. Mash the pulp well with a fork, and, if you are going to serve the pie hot, add the butter. (Butter goes grainy when cold.)
- Cool the pie mixture before using.

- While the pie mixture is cooling, you can make the pastry. Rub the fats into the flour and mix the icing sugar well in. Mix to a dough with the cold water and lemon juice. Cut the dough into 2 pieces.
- Flour a pastry board or clean work surface and flour your rolling pin. Roll out each piece of pastry to fit an 8 or 9-inch (20 or 23-cm) pie plate.

- Lightly butter the plate. Press in one piece of pastry letting it overlap by about ¼–½ inch (.5–1 cm).
- Prick all over with a large fork.
- Bake this blind at Gas Mark 7, Electricity 425°F or 220°C for 10–12 minutes. Remove. Cool. Trim off the cooked pastry.
- Pile in the apple filling. Beat the egg and brush it on the edge. Fit the rolled out lid. *Press* the edges together raw to cooked.
- Brush all over with beaten egg. Dredge with caster sugar.
- Bake at Gas Mark 6, Electricity 400°F or 200°C for 15–20 minutes.
- Allow to cool. Cover with plastic film and refrigerate.
- Serve cold, or reheat at Gas Mark 6, Electricity 400°F or 200°C for 10–15 minutes.

Accompaniments
- Drink with it a glass of light Madeira or Sauternes. Or, as in Yorkshire where cheese is often served with apple pie, iced white port.

Madeira Syllabub

*T*his rich dessert is to be eaten in small quantities. The syllabubs can be made the day before. If you do so, you will notice that the mixture will thicken fully acquiring a mousse-like texture. This in no way affects the flavour: it's just 'different'.

Ingredients

1 large orange
2 ozs (50 grams) sugar (*or* 3 ozs/75 grams if you have a sweet tooth)
¼ pint (150 ml) dryish Madeira *or*

Amontillado sherry
2 Tablespoons brandy
tip of 1 teaspoon ground cinnamon
½ pint (275 ml) double cream

Advance preparation
(15 + minutes)

- Take the orange and grate off the zest, by standing the grater on a plate and making short downward movements on the fine-toothed blade, turning the orange slightly after each cut. Avoid grating off the bitter white pith. Scrape the oily zest into a 2-pint (1-litre) bowl or basin. Cut the orange in half, squeeze well and strain the juice through a sieve into the same bowl.
- Add the sugar and wine, the brandy and the cinnamon. Cover with plastic film and leave to soak for a few hours, or overnight.
- In a second bowl, using a hand (balloon) whisk, stir round and start beating the cream until it just begins to 'ribbon', working from the outside of the bowl to the centre.
- Start to pour the softened sugar, wine and juice mixture into the

half-whipped cream, stirring and whisking as you do this. When all the juice is added, continue calmly whisking the cream until it 'ribbons' well and just stands in soft peaks when you draw the whisk through and up out of the mixture. The cream should 'fall back' readily.
- Ladle or spoon the syllabub into six nice small wine glasses (about 5 fl ozs/150 ml size). Wipe the edges clean. Cover each glass with a small piece of plastic film. Stand them on a large plate or tray and refrigerate until ready to serve.

Accompaniments

- Serve with a Petticoat Tail Shortbread, Langue de Chat or a Boudoir biscuit.
- Stand each glass on a small doilyed plate and serve with a teaspoon.
- Madeira or a cream sherry will accompany this well.

Basics

Contents

● ● ●

Practical Tips

How to Hard-Boil Eggs

- Put six eggs in a pan just large enough to contain them in one layer with ½ inch (1 cm) of space between them.
- Cover the eggs with *cold* water, no more than ½ inch (1 cm) over their tops.
- Bring to the boil over a good heat: as soon as the water is boiling, lower the heat so that the eggs are boiling gently. This will take 15 minutes from start to finish.

- Pour off the boiling water. Run cold water over the eggs for at least 15 minutes to cool them down, whilst cracking the shells against each other to release hot gases which cause the dark ring often seen round egg yolks.
- Shell them under running water. Pat them dry, and store them, refrigerated, in a lidded plastic container, or a sealed plastic bag.

How to Separate an Egg Yolk

There are two common ways of doing this, so you can choose for yourself. Any sane man will use Method 1. Most women use Method 2.

Method 1
- Carefully break an egg into a small basin.
- Slide the second and third fingers under the yolk (watch that your nails don't pierce the membrane) and lift it out of the basin, letting the white fall slowly away.
- If the eggs are newly laid, you'll have to squeeze the heavy glutinous part of the white very gently off the yolk.

Method 2
- Crack the egg on the edge of a basin.

- Hold the two halves together over the basin and gently open them up, then tip the yolk from one half to the other and back again, allowing the white to escape between the shells. This method is less messy than the one above.

- For both methods, discard the white. If you pour it down the sink, help it on its way with cold water. If you use hot, it will solidify in the waste pipe.

Basic Mayonnaise

*M*ayonnaise will not keep indefinitely, just 7–10 days, but home-made mayonnaise is much preferable to the shop-bought variety, if you can find the time to make it. This recipe will make 1½ pints (825 ml).

Ingredients

6 egg yolks
salt
1 teaspoon dry mustard

freshly ground white pepper
1 pint (570 ml) oil (half soy oil, half olive oil) *at room temperature*
2 Tablespoons wine vinegar
single cream, for thinning if necessary

*P*reparation

(20 minutes)

- Separate the yolks from the egg whites (see p.129).
- Put the yolks into a round-bottomed basin. This is essential as you need to collect and control the yolks within a small area. Add the salt, mustard and a little pepper and work these with a balloon whisk, until they are really thick and sticky.
- Have the oil in a jug, then, using a teaspoon, add the first few drops of oil to the egg mixture, whisking vigorously. Beat this well in before adding the next few drops. It is essential to take care in the early stages of mayonnaise making—if you are meticulous at the beginning, you will have no trouble later.
- After the first Tablespoonful or so has been added slowly, you can start to add the oil more quickly—experience will teach you just when this can be done. As soon as the emulsion starts to reject the oil (this is quite different from curdling) add a little vinegar and beat until it is creamy again. Mayonnaise is curdled when the solid part goes thin and flecky. If this happens, you must start again with a single egg yolk and work the curdled mayonnaise into it drop by drop. Sometimes a Tablespoon of boiling water added to the curdled mayonnaise works.
- Keep the mayonnaise as stiff as your arm will allow! By this I mean that if you have a strong arm you will be able to have mayonnaise as thick as butter, which can virtually be cut with a knife. When a more liquid mayonnaise is needed, thin down

130

with single cream, vinegar or cold water (or a combination of all three); water gives a blander result than vinegar, cream adds richness.

- Store in a cool, but not cold, place. If it begins to look oily, add a spoonful of boiling water and whisk until creamy again.

*V*arations

- The finished mayonnaise can be flavoured with ketchup, sherry, lemon juice, brandy, Worcestershire sauce etc.

How to Snip Chives

*I*f you buy chives they come either in bundles held with a rubber band, or loose in small polystyrene trays, covered with plastic film. In which case, slip a rubber band round them.

- Slide the band down to the *thin* end of the herb.
- Discard any brown, withered or damaged bits.
- Rinse the bundle under cold running water. Pat dry with a paper kitchen towel.
- Take a teacup or plastic container. Using kitchen scissors, snip them small into the cup.
- Store, covered, in the refrigerator, until ready to use. Chives can be prepared 4–6 hours in advance.

How to Chop an Onion

- Take the onion. Cut a ⅛-inch (.25-cm) sliver from the base and top of the onion and discard. Remove the outer skin and the second layer if it has any brown on it.
- Stand it upright on a board. Cut the onion in half, downwards.
- Lay each half flat on the board and cut each half lengthways into 4 strips, then into 4 crossways, giving approx. ½-inch (1-cm) squares. Fully separate the pieces with your fingers. Scrape on to a plate till ready for use.

131

Parsley:
How to Snip It
and How to Chop It

*B*ought parsley often looks drab and limp in the shops. If it is totally so, do not buy it, nor should you buy it if it looks yellow and bleached. However, in warm weather, or towards the end of the day, in shops where the owner hasn't the wit to keep it in a bucket of water, it will look wilted. This is O.K., but get him (or her) to *give* it to you.

When you get home, immerse the parsley totally in a bucket or bowl of water until it livens up. Shake it dry, using a vigorous movement, so do this outside or over the bath!

Sometimes parsley is snipped, sometimes finely chopped. There is a subtle difference worth noting.

*H*ow to Snip It

- Using scissors, patiently clip off the florets discarding the major stalks. Leave the little ones on. Put the florets into a straight-sided large mug or other similar container, and snip away until it is as fine as you want it.
- Mint can be snipped the same way.

*H*ow to Chop It

- Put the florets, with a little water, into a blender and chop it this way. Scrape and pour into a strainer. Scrape the chopped parsley into the corner of a clean tea towel. Gather the fabric round it, and twist it dry over the sink. Don't let go until you have the towel over a plate. Carefully release the squeezed parsley on to the plate and use or transfer it to a small cup or plastic container, and store covered with plastic film. Parsley can be chopped the night before and stored, covered, refrigerated.

132

Bread Sauce

Ingredients

2 ozs (50 grams) onion
½ small clove garlic
1 oz (25 grams) butter

1½ ozs (40 grams) white breadcrumbs
⅓ pint (190 ml) rich milk
¼ pint (150 ml) double cream
¼ teaspoon ground mace
salt

*A*dvance preparation
(45 minutes)

- Skin and chop the onion (see p.131).
- Peel and crush the garlic.
- In the top of a double boiler directly over a low heat, melt the butter without allowing it to colour.
- Soften the onion in this, also without allowing it to colour.
- Fill the base of the double boiler with water and replace the top in it.
- Add the milk, breadcrumbs, mace and garlic and simmer, covered for 30–40 minutes.

- The sauce can be made a day or two in advance, in which case pour a Tablespoon or two of melted butter over the surface to prevent a skin from forming.
- Re-heat in the double boiler, beat well with a balloon whisk as the sauce will have thickened up when cold.

*F*inishing touches
- Stir in the cream, re-heat in a double boiler, or in a basin over hot water and serve. The sauce should be of a creamy consistency, not thick. If it is too thick, add some more hot milk.

Parsley Sauce

Ingredients

2 large bunches parsley (to make 2 Teacups finely chopped)
3 ozs (75 grams) unsalted butter

1 heaped Tablespoon plain white flour
½ pint (275 ml) milk
½ pint (275 ml) single cream (or all milk)
salt and milled white (*or* black) pepper

*A*dvance preparation time
(10 minutes)
- Chop the parsley.

*L*ast-minute cooking
(12 minutes)
- In a 2-pint (or 1-litre) pan, over a

low heat, gently melt the butter without letting it brown at the edges. Swirl the pan around as you do this.

- Using a small balloon whisk, whisk in the flour. Gradually incorporate the milk, a little at a time, and whisking briskly as you do so: still over a low heat.
- Allow the sauce to come to the boil, whisking gently to ensure a smooth texture. Let the sauce bubble quietly for 3–4 minutes. It will be thickish.

- Now pour in the cream. Season to taste with salt and white pepper. (Black pepper leaves specks.)
- Allow the sauce to bubble again. It should be smooth. Strain it into a 2-pint (1-litre) basin arranged over a pan of *almost* boiling water.
- Stir in the parsley. Cut a circle of paper to fit the surface of the sauce. Butter this well to the edges; this will stop a skin forming whilst the sauce is kept hot.

How to Knife-peel and Segment Citrus Fruit

- Stand the piece of citrus fruit on a kitchen board. Have a few pieces of kitchen paper to hand to mop up any wayward juices which may flow as you work.
- Have a small glass or china basin to hand.
- Using a serrated knife (not saw-toothed), start by cutting ¼ inch (.5 cm) off the top *and* bottom of the fruit.
- Continue cutting off slivers of skin in this way until a good inch (2 cm) surface of the flesh is exposed at *both* ends of the fruit. Discard the skin as you work.
- Next, starting at the top right-hand side of the fruit, cut *around*, *down* and *under* to reveal the flesh. The first slice is the key to it all: once the flesh is revealed, use this revealed cut edge as a guide, following it as you cut.

- Continue cutting in ½-inch (1-cm) wide strips until the fruit is completely peeled. Shave off any bits of pith which may have escaped your knife.
- Now hold the fruit in your left hand, over the basin, and carefully cut between the membrane of each segment, allowing the segment to fall into the basin as you cut.
- Halfway through you may find it easier to place the fruit on the board and cut against this.
- Squeeze any juice into the basin from the remaining débris, and discard the membrane.
- Alternatively proceed up to completely taking the outer skin off, then cut the fruit in half (top to bottom, not equatorwise), and slice each half across thinly, into semi-circular pieces.

How to Skin, De-seed and Chop a Tomato

- Bring a 6-pint (or 3-litre) saucepan of water to the boil, and have a large bowl of cold water by the stove.
- Remove the stalks from the tomatoes. With a small, pointed knife, stab a cross in the base of each tomato. (This will enable you to remove the skins more easily.) With a slotted spoon quickly immerse them into the bubbling water. Leave for 10 seconds, when you will see the slit skin starting to peel back. Remove from saucepan and immerse in the bowl of cold water. Pull off skins and discard them.
- Cut each tomato in half, equatorwise; press the seeds and pulp out of the cavities with your thumb and discard them. Cut the halves into quarters, then chop.

Stocks

Basic Rich Brown Beef Stock

*I*t is always useful to have a supply of home-made beef stock by you in the deep freezer. This makes 4 pints (2.3 litres).

Ingredients

2 lbs (1.3 kg) mixed marrowbones and other beef bones, sawn into manageable pieces
3 lbs (1.3 kg) shin of beef
2 Tablespoons olive oil *or* soy oil
8 ozs (225 grams) carrots
2 sticks celery
1 leek
4 ozs (100 grams) field *or* flat-cap mushrooms
1 pint (570 ml) Burgundy-type red wine
a fresh bouquet garni *or* commercial sachets
1 lb (450 grams) tomatoes
1 teaspoon salt
1 Tablespoon black peppercorns
5–6 pints (2.9–3.4 litres) cold water
4 ozs (100 grams) onion

☰ Advance preparation
(20 minutes)

- Trim *all* the fat from the beef, and cut the meat into 2-inch (5-cm) pieces.
- Skin, deseed and chop the tomatoes (see p.135)
- Trim and roughly chop the rest of the vegetables, except the mushrooms which go in whole and the onion which should be peeled and cut in half.

☰ Cooking
(3 hours)

- Place the bones in a roasting tin and brown in pre-heated oven (Gas Mark 8, Electricity 450°F or 230°C), turning them with tongs to ensure they are well coloured. This can take 45 minutes to 1 hour.
- Remove the bones and place on one side on a tray. Transfer the roasting tin to the top of the cooker and brown the shin in the residue fats on all sides, over a fierce heat, working with a manageable batch at a time, and stirring with a wooden spatula to prevent burning.
- Heat the oil in a large saucepan until smoking. Add the carrots and celery and brown over a high heat, stirring with a wooden spatula to ensure even colouring and no burning. Lower the heat to almost minimal. Add the bones, meat and all the other ingredients apart from the onion, pouring in sufficient cold water to cover. (Discard any fatty residues.)
- Bring to the boil very slowly in order to extract all the goodness from the bones and meat.
- Meanwhile, brown the onion by placing the halves, cut-side down, in a dry frying pan over a low heat. Allow them to brown gently but completely. They should be caramelized but not burnt.
- Once the stock is boiling, add the browned onion and keep at a steady boil, not just simmering. Be careful, however, as a rapid boil will cloud the stock. Cook, uncovered, for 3 hours, skimming off any scum which rises to the surface during this lengthy process.
- Cool. Decant the stock slowly through a sieve lined with a piece of kitchen paper.
- Store in 8 ½-pint (275-ml) plastic containers in the deep freezer for easy use.

*H*ome-made stock tastes so much better than any made from commercial cubes, so if you do have the time to make it, it is worthwhile, for it can be stored in the deep freezer for later use. This recipe makes 3 pints (1.7 litres).

Ingredients

4 ozs (100 grams) carrots
2 large leeks (white part only)
2 stalks celery
4 ozs (100 grams) white-cap mushrooms
3-lb (1.3-kg) chicken (*or* boiling fowl)
1½–2 lbs (675–900 grams) knuckle of

veal, chopped into manageable pieces
1 Tablespoon butter *or* soy oil
1 bouquet garni sachet
1 pint (570 ml) dry white wine
3 pints (1.7 litres) or more cold water
2 teaspoons salt
12 white peppercorns

*A*dvance preparation
(20 minutes)

- Peel and slice the carrots. Trim, wash and finely slice the leeks and celery. Rub clean and slice the mushrooms.

*C*ooking
(2 hours 10 minutes)

- Melt the butter in a large pan without browning it. Add the carrots, leeks and celery, cover and soften over a low heat, without browning, for 12–15 minutes.
- Add the chicken, knuckle pieces, mushrooms and bouquet garni. Pour the wine and water over to cover. Add the salt and peppercorns, then bring to the boil *slowly*. Adjust the heat, so

that the liquid is boiling, but only gently so. Rapid boiling creates a cloudy stock.

- Boil at this gentle pace for 2 hours, taking the chicken out after 1½ hours and skimming the surface of any scum which may collect. (You can of course use the chicken—see at the end of the instructions.)
- Cool, then decant the clear stock into a large bowl through a sieve lined with clean muslin or paper towel. Be patient, let the stock trickle through at its own pace: do not be tempted to press it through. Change the paper, or rinse the muslin from time to time to rid it of any sediments.
- If you are not using any immediately then make up 6

plastic containers holding ½ pint (275 ml) each, and freeze these for easy use in the future.
- Use up the chicken or boiling fowl in a Vinaigrette (see p.103), or in a chicken and pasta salad (p.52). It will curry well, too.

Dressings

Basic Rich French Dressing

*T*his recipe will make ½ pint (275 ml). The dressing will keep for months in the fridge.

Ingredients

1 rounded teaspoon mild French mustard
scant ½ teaspoon salt
scant ½ teaspoon milled black *or* mixed pepper
1 teaspoon *caster* sugar
⅛ pint (75 ml) red *or* white wine vinegar
⅛ pint (75 ml) rich olive oil
¼ pint (150 ml) soy oil

Preparation
(2 minutes)
- Put all the ingredients into a screw-top jar, or a jar with a ground glass stopper, and shake vigorously until well emulsified.
- Use immediately, or store, refrigerated, until ready for use.
- *Do not store once you have added garlic or herbs.*

Garlic Dressing

Method
- To each ½ pint (275 ml) of Basic French Dressing add: 1 small peeled, crushed clove of garlic, just before or 1 hour before using.
- Shake well.

Herb Dressing

*T*here is little need to resort to dried herbs, so I do not recommend them.

To each ½ pint (275 ml) Basic French Dressing add:

1 dessertspoon finely snipped chives (p.131)

1 dessertspoon snipped, not over-so, parsley (p.132)

1 dessertspoon of *one* of the following:
basil
mint
tarragon
marjoram
dill

- Add a small clove of crushed garlic if liked.

Savoury Butters

Tomato, Curry and Orange Butter

Ingredients

6 ozs (175 grams) unsalted butter, softened

1 level teaspoon salt

2 Tablespoons tomato purée

1 teaspoon finely grated orange zest

1 heaped teaspoon *mild* Madras curry powder *or* paste

Method
- Mix all the ingredients together in a liquidiser.
- Rub through a fine-meshed sieve, and put them into wax or plastic cartons.

- Chill until required in either the freezer or the refrigerator.
- When ready to use, take the butter out of the freezer or refrigerator and allow it to come to room temperature.

139

Lemon and Parsley Butter

Method
- Make up one batch of Lemon Butter as above.
- After sieving, add 1 teacup of freshly picked, very finely chopped parsley (see p.132).

Mint Butter

Ingredients

6 ozs (175 grams) unsalted butter, softened
18–20 large mint leaves, rinsed

2 teaspoons lemon juice
1 level teaspoons salt
1 level teaspoons sugar

Method
- Make a fine purée of all the ingredients in a liquidiser.
- Rub through a fine-meshed sieve.
- Pack and store as above.

Mixed Herb Butter

Ingredients

6 ozs (175 grams) unsalted butter, softened
4 Tablespoons each of the following fresh herbs:
    parsley, fennel fronts, chervil and chives, *or* tarragon, chives and flat-leaf parsley
half clove of garlic, crushed
1 teaspoon lemon juice
1 teaspoon salt
freshly ground white pepper to taste

Method
- Finely chop the herbs and blend together all the ingredients.
- Store and pack as above.